Math

Grade 3

Printed in the U.S.A.

ISBN 978-0-544-26821-0

 4 5 6 7 8 9 10   0928   22 21 20 19 18 17 16 15

4500523808   B C D E F G

Core Skills Math

GRADE 3

Table of Contents

© Houghton Mifflin Harcourt Publishing Company

Common Core State Standards for Mathematics Correlation Chart

Operations and Algebraic Thinking

Represent and solve problems involving multiplication and division.

3.OA.1	27, 28, 29, 30, 31, 32, 38, 44, 45
3.OA.2	57, 58, 59, 60
3.OA.3	74, 75
3.OA.4	76, 77

Understand properties of multiplication and the relationship between multiplication and division.

3.OA.5	49, 50, 51
3.OA.6	68

Multiply and divide within 100.

3.OA.7	33, 34, 35, 36, 37, 39, 40, 41, 42, 43, 46, 55, 56, 61, 62, 63, 64, 65, 66, 67, 69, 70, 71, 72, 73, 79

Solve problems involving the four operations, and identify and explain patterns in arithmetic.

3.OA.8 *Supporting Skills*	141, 142, 143 139, 140
3.OA.9	4, 47, 48, 78

Number and Operations in Base Ten

Use place value understanding and properties of operations to perform multi-digit arithmetic.

3.NBT.1	136, 137, 138
3.NBT.2	1, 2, 3, 5, 6, 7, 8, 9, 10, 11, 12, 13, 14, 15, 16, 17, 18, 19
3.NBT.3	52, 53, 54

Number and Operations—Fractions

Develop understanding of fractions as numbers.

3.NF.1	118, 119, 122, 123, 124
3.NF.2	
3.NF.2.a	125
3.NF.2.b	125
3.NF.3	
3.NF.3.a	126

v

3.NF.3.b	127, 128, 129, 130
3.NF.3.c	131
3.NF.3.d	132, 133, 134, 135

Measurement and Data

Solve problems involving measurement and estimation of intervals of time, liquid volumes, and masses of objects.

3.MD.1	20, 21, 22, 23, 24, 25, 26
3.MD.2 *Supporting Skills*	113, 114, 116, 117 115

Represent and interpret data.

3.MD.3	100, 101, 102, 103, 104, 105, 106, 107, 108, 109, 110
3.MD.4 *Supporting Skills*	112 111

Geometric measurement: understand concepts of area and relate area to multiplication and to addition.

3.MD.5	
3.MD.5.a	92
3.MD.5.b	93
3.MD.6	93, 94
3.MD.7	
3.MD.7.a	95
3.MD.7.b	96, 97
3.MD.7.c	98
3.MD.7.d	98

Geometric measurement: recognize perimeter as an attribute of plane figures and distinguish between linear and area measures.

3.MD.8 *Supporting Skills*	85, 87, 88, 89, 90, 91, 99 86

Geometry

Reason with shapes and their attributes.

3.G.1	80, 81, 82, 83, 84
3.G.2	120, 121

Counting On and Make a Ten

Find the sum.

| 1. | 3
 + 5 | 2. | 7
 + 4 | 3. | 6
 + 5 | 4. | 8
 + 4 | 5. | 9
 + 6 | 6. | 8
 + 3 | 7. | 5
 + 8 |

| 8. | 7
 + 7 | 9. | 6
 + 7 | 10. | 9
 + 2 | 11. | 9
 + 3 | 12. | 8
 + 2 | 13. | 7
 + 5 | 14. | 6
 + 6 |

15. $3 + 6 =$ _____   16. $2 + 9 =$ _____   17. $8 + 8 =$ _____

18. $5 + 5 =$ _____   19. $8 + 7 =$ _____   20. $4 + 6 =$ _____

MIXED APPLICATIONS

Solve. Label your answer.

21. Ben had 8 fish in his aquarium. He bought 7 more fish. How many fish does Ben have in his aquarium now?

22. Meg sees 5 rainbow fish at the aquarium, but 3 other rainbow fish are hidden. How many rainbow fish are there?

_____

_____

VISUAL THINKING

This number line shows $3 + 5 = 8$.

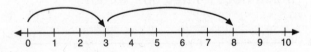

Match each addition sentence to a number line.

23. $4 + 5 = 9$

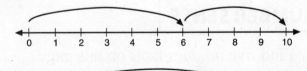

24. $6 + 4 = 10$

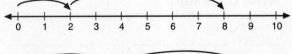

25. $2 + 6 = 8$

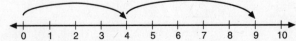

1

Doubles and Doubles Plus One

Find the sum.

1. 3 + 3	**2.** 7 + 8	**3.** 6 + 9	**4.** 8 + 5	**5.** 9 + 8	**6.** 2 + 3	**7.** 5 + 4

8. 5 + 5	**9.** 6 + 7	**10.** 3 + 8	**11.** 2 + 2	**12.** 8 + 7	**13.** 4 + 7	**14.** 6 + 6

15. $5 + 8 =$ _____   **16.** $6 + 5 =$ _____   **17.** $4 + 4 =$ _____

18. $8 + 9 =$ _____   **19.** $5 + 9 =$ _____   **20.** $7 + 7 =$ _____

21. $9 + 7 =$ _____   **22.** $7 + 6 =$ _____   **23.** $9 + 9 =$ _____

24. $8 + 8 =$ _____   **25.** $4 + 5 =$ _____   **26.** $8 + 6 =$ _____

27. $5 + 5 =$ _____   **28.** $6 + 6 =$ _____   **29.** $7 + 8 =$ _____

MIXED APPLICATIONS

30. Kate bought a 6-ounce box of dog treats. A large box is double the weight of the 6-ounce box. How much does a large box weigh?

_____

31. Kate got her dog when he was 7 months old. That was 3 months ago. How old is Kate's dog now?

_____

NUMBER SENSE

32. Find five *doubles* facts on this page. Write their sums.

____ ____ ____ ____ ____

33. Find five *doubles plus one* facts. Write their sums.

____ ____ ____ ____ ____

Counting Back and Counting Up

Find the difference.

| **1.** 8
$\underline{-\,5}$ | **2.** 7
$\underline{-\,3}$ | **3.** 6
$\underline{-\,2}$ | **4.** 10
$\underline{-\,3}$ | **5.** 9
$\underline{-\,7}$ | **6.** 8
$\underline{-\,1}$ | **7.** 5
$\underline{-\,4}$ |

| **8.** 7
$\underline{-\,4}$ | **9.** 6
$\underline{-\,3}$ | **10.** 9
$\underline{-\,6}$ | **11.** 9
$\underline{-\,4}$ | **12.** 8
$\underline{-\,7}$ | **13.** 7
$\underline{-\,6}$ | **14.** 6
$\underline{-\,1}$ |

15. $7 - 5 =$ _____   **16.** $10 - 8 =$ _____   **17.** $8 - 1 =$ _____

18. $9 - 4 =$ _____   **19.** $6 - 4 =$ _____   **20.** $10 - 9 =$ _____

MIXED APPLICATIONS

21. Al's cat had 7 kittens. He gave away all of the kittens but 2. How many kittens did Al give away?

_____

22. Rosa bought 6 cans of turkey and 3 cans of liver for her kittens. How many more cans of turkey than liver did Rosa buy?

_____

EVERYDAY MATH CONNECTION

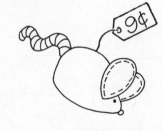
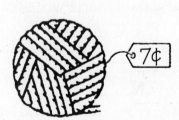

23. The pet store is having a sale on all cat toys. Every item is 3¢ off the marked price. Find the sale price of each item.

rattle _____   catnip mouse _____   yarn ball _____

Number Patterns

Find the sum. Then write the related addition sentence.

1. $9 + 2 =$ _____

__ + __ = _____

2. $3 + 10 =$ _____

__ + __ = _____

3. $8 + 9 =$ _____

__ + __ = _____

4. $4 + 7 =$ _____

__ + __ = _____

5. $6 + 7 =$ _____

__ + __ = _____

6. $0 + 4 =$ _____

__ + __ = _____

7. $3 + 6 =$ _____

__ + __ = _____

8. $7 + 5 =$ _____

__ + __ = _____

9. $9 + 6 =$ _____

__ + __ = _____

Is the sum even or odd? Write *even* or *odd*.

10. $5 + 2$ _____

11. $6 + 4$ _____

12. $1 + 0$ _____

13. $5 + 5$ _____

14. $3 + 8$ _____

15. $7 + 7$ _____

PROBLEM SOLVING

16. Ada writes $10 + 8 = 18$ on the board. Maria wants to use the Commutative Property of Addition to rewrite Ada's addition sentence. What number sentence should Maria write?

_____

17. Jackson says he has an odd number of model cars. He has 6 cars on one shelf and 8 cars on another shelf. Is Jackson correct? Explain.

_____

_____

_____

4

Adding 1- and 2-Digit Numbers

Estimate the sum by rounding.

1. 42 + 37	**2.** 86 + 12	**3.** 39 + 56	**4.** 21 +69	**5.** 68 +12	**6.** 19 + 23

7. 61 + 3	**8.** 22 + 9	**9.** 37 + 21	**10.** 42 + 11	**11.** 18 + 68	**12.** 27 + 33

Find the sum.

13. 62 + 15	**14.** 79 + 2	**15.** 23 + 46	**16.** 35 + 33	**17.** 23 + 9	**18.** 41 + 28

19. 68 + 21	**20.** 52 + 27	**21.** 63 + 26	**22.** 44 + 45	**23.** 82 + 9	**24.** 67 + 12

MIXED APPLICATIONS

25. It takes 38 minutes in the morning and 42 minutes in the evening to feed the seals. To the nearest ten, how many minutes does feeding the seals take?

26. The monkeys snack on 18 bananas and 9 apples each afternoon. How many pieces of fruit do the monkeys eat in all?

EVERYDAY MATH CONNECTION

27. Marielle buys two small bags of peanuts for $0.35 each. George buys one large bag for $0.75. Who spends more money? How much more?

Adding 2-Digit Numbers

Estimate the sum by rounding.

1.	39 + 47	2.	76 + 19	3.	58 + 39	4.	90 + 11	5.	76 + 41	6.	48 + 87

Find the sum.

7.	78 + 21	8.	55 + 94	9.	9 + 97	10.	85 + 34	11.	27 + 72	12.	43 + 76

13.	51 + 33	14.	65 + 53	15.	91 + 43	16.	41 + 37	17.	21 + 98	18.	57 + 82

19.	43 + 55	20.	32 + 46	21.	48 + 91	22.	32 + 26	23.	33 + 85	24.	13 + 52

MIXED APPLICATIONS

25. The dolphin show is 27 minutes long. The seal show lasts 25 minutes. How long are both shows combined?

26. The animal trainer feeds the porpoises two buckets of fish. Each bucket contains 87 fish. How many fish do they eat in all?

LOGICAL REASONING

27. Two addends combine to make a sum of about 80. One addend is 56. Is the other addend less than or greater than 56?

28. Three addends combine to make a sum of about 100. Two of the addends are less than 20. Is the third addend less than or greater than 50?

Subtracting 1- and 2-Digit Numbers

Estimate the difference by rounding. Show your work.

1. 98 ____	2. 51 ____	3. 82 ____	4. 72 ____
− 29 − ____	− 18 − ____	− 41 − ____	− 8 − ____
____	____	____	____

Find the difference.

5. 87	6. 75	7. 39	8. 96	9. 87	10. 49
− 63	− 54	− 17	− 53	− 27	− 38

11. 98	12. 78	13. 78	14. 88	15. 68	16. 39
− 42	− 41	− 10	− 78	− 40	− 24

MIXED APPLICATIONS

17. Tickets to the circus cost $15 for adults and $8 for children. How much will it cost for a family of two adults and one child to go to the circus?

_____

18. Bill can buy popcorn for 32¢ or peanuts for 75¢. How much more do peanuts cost than popcorn?

_____

EVERYDAY MATH CONNECTION

peanuts 39¢   popcorn 25¢   drink 15¢   taco 50¢

19. Choose two different snacks to buy. Circle them.

What is the total cost? _____
How much change would you get from 95¢? _____

Unit 2
Core Skills Math, Grade 3

Subtracting with Zeros

Estimate the difference.

1. 60 − 29	2. 50 − 11	3. 40 − 32	4. 90 − 58	5. 80 − 79	6. 70 − 41

Find the difference. Check by adding.

7. 90 _____ − 23 + _____ _____	8. 50 _____ − 18 + _____ _____	9. 80 _____ − 46 + _____ _____	10. 70 _____ − 63 + _____ _____
11. 40 _____ − 17 + _____ _____	12. 60 _____ − 27 + _____ _____	13. 30 _____ − 19 + _____ _____	14. 90 _____ − 45 + _____ _____

MIXED APPLICATIONS

15. The parrot house contains 56 parrots and 37 other colorful birds. How many birds are in the parrot house?

16. In the flamingo garden, 17 of the 40 pink birds are wading in the shallow pond. How many flamingos are not wading?

SCIENCE CONNECTION

17. Flamingos usually lay a single egg in a shallow hole at the top of a mound of mud. The parents take turns sitting on the egg to keep it warm. Last year at the wildlife park, one flamingo egg took 27 days to hatch and another egg took 32 days. What is the difference between the hatching times of the two eggs?

8

Addition and Subtraction Practice

Find the sum or difference.

1. $\begin{array}{r} 23 \\ + 46 \end{array}$	2. $\begin{array}{r} 54 \\ + 65 \end{array}$	3. $\begin{array}{r} 98 \\ - 47 \end{array}$	4. $\begin{array}{r} 86 \\ - 21 \end{array}$	5. $\begin{array}{r} 91 \\ + 18 \end{array}$	6. $\begin{array}{r} 39 \\ - 7 \end{array}$

7. $\begin{array}{r} 43 \\ + 56 \end{array}$	8. $\begin{array}{r} 29 \\ - 12 \end{array}$	9. $\begin{array}{r} 86 \\ - 51 \end{array}$	10. $\begin{array}{r} 73 \\ + 73 \end{array}$	11. $\begin{array}{r} 87 \\ - 43 \end{array}$	12. $\begin{array}{r} 21 \\ + 98 \end{array}$

MIXED APPLICATIONS

Use the table to solve.

13. Which circus toy is the best seller?

_____

14. Which toy is least popular?

_____

Toy	Number Sold
balloon	2,508
stuffed lion	1,897
banner	980
circus visor	2,256

15. Which toys have sales of about 2,000?

_____

16. Put the sales of stuffed lions, banners, and circus visors in order from highest to lowest.

_____

_____

WRITER'S CORNER

17. Make up your own question about the data in the table.

_____

_____

3-Digit Addition with Regrouping

Find the sum. Regroup if you need to.

1.   268
  + 409
	2. 435
	  + 943
		3. 119
		  + 605
			4. 34
			  + 128
				5. 263
				  + 144

6.   328
  + 851
	7. 768
	  + 126
		8. 418
		  + 475
			9. 689
			  + 410
				10. 254
				  + 314

11.   209
  + 68
	12. 323
	  + 524
		13. 353
		  + 139
			14. 220
			  + 719
				15. 293
				  + 546

16. In which exercises were the ones regrouped?

_____

17. In which exercises were the tens regrouped?

_____

18. In which exercises were the hundreds regrouped?

_____

19. In which exercises were none of the places regrouped?

_____

VISUAL THINKING

Find the sum. You may use place-value models to help you.

20.

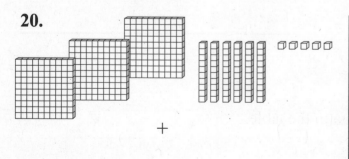

+

= _____

21.

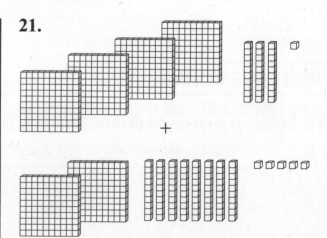

+

= _____

Name _____ Date _____

Addition with Regrouping More Than Once

Regroup more than once to add. Write the regrouped numbers.

1. 11
365
+ 285
650

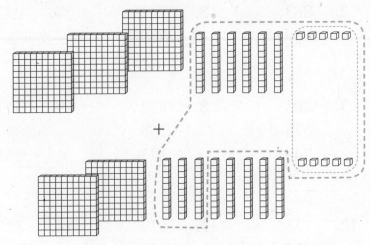

	5 hundreds	14 tens	10 ones
Regroup ones.	5 hundreds	___ tens	0 ones
Regroup tens.	___ hundreds	5 tens	0 ones

Use place-value models to add. Regroup if you need to.

2. 247 + 683	**3.** 578 + 243	**4.** 490 + 247	**5.** 146 + 374	**6.** 764 + 85

7. 234 + 368	**8.** 607 + 409	**9.** 583 + 75	**10.** 35 + 167	**11.** 872 + 500

NUMBER SENSE

12. What number can you make with
7 hundreds 9 tens 10 ones?

13. What number can you make with
2 hundreds 9 tens 14 ones?

_____   _____

3-Digit Addition with Two or Three Addends

Find the sum.

1.	497 + 628	**2.**	283 + 684	**3.**	741 + 759	**4.**	942 + 89	**5.**	987 + 702

6.	468 120 + 371	**7.**	203 75 + 849	**8.**	452 268 + 173	**9.**	511 19 + 265	**10.**	496 265 + 306

11.	321 450 + 147	**12.**	53 625 + 219	**13.**	679 102 + 328	**14.**	825 319 + 89	**15.**	209 425 + 85

MIXED APPLICATIONS

16. Train Treats sells 547 rolls and 665 bagels each morning to people riding the train to work. How many rolls and bagels is this?

17. Train Treats orders 284 boxes of herbal tea. A supply of 549 boxes is already in stock. How many boxes will there be when the order comes in?

HEALTH CONNECTION

18. Ming wants to do 100 push-ups each week. She had done 85 push-ups after 6 days, and she did 20 more on the seventh day. Did Ming reach her goal?

19. Ron runs around the 440-yard track with his dad twice in one day. He runs it one time the next day. How many yards does Ron run in both days?

Subtracting from 3-Digit Numbers

Find the difference.

1.	165 − 52	**2.**	489 − 46	**3.**	256 − 46	**4.**	698 − 37	**5.**	362 − 40
6.	123 − 11	**7.**	596 − 62	**8.**	247 − 14	**9.**	498 − 87	**10.**	166 − 40
11.	239 − 17	**12.**	153 − 21	**13.**	419 − 16	**14.**	367 − 32	**15.**	384 − 80

MIXED APPLICATIONS

16. Saul rode his bicycle 118 miles one week. The next week he rode 16 fewer miles. How many miles did he ride the second week?

_____

17. Tasha practices piano 225 minutes each week. She practices 20 minutes on the first day. How many minutes more will she practice the rest of the week?

_____

VISUAL THINKING

18. Annika made two models that show 243. Which model should she use if she wants to show how to subtract 8? Circle the model.

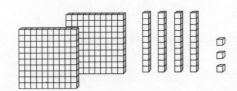   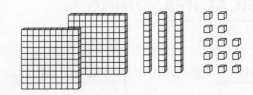

Subtracting with Regrouping Tens

Find the difference. Regroup tens if you need to.

1.

Not enough ones

H	T	O
3	4	6
− 1	2	9

Regroup and subtract.

H	T	O
	3	16
3	4̶	6̶
− 1	2	9

2.

Not enough ones

H	T	O
6	8	0
− 4	1	5

Regroup and subtract.

H	T	O
	7	10
6	8̶	0̶
− 4	1	5

3.
```
  870
− 543
```

4.
```
  965
− 247
```

5.
```
  785
− 183
```

6.
```
  973
−  48
```

7.
```
  697
− 160
```

8.
```
  375
− 125
```

9.
```
  892
− 537
```

10.
```
  660
− 435
```

11.
```
  897
− 369
```

12.
```
  768
− 265
```

MIXED APPLICATIONS

13. A taxi driver travels 465 miles in Week 1 and 582 miles in Week 2. How many more miles does he drive in Week 2?

_____

14. There were 367 people at one concert and 505 people at another concert. How many people were at the concerts?

_____

LOGICAL REASONING

Circle exercises that have estimated sums or differences greater than 500. Then use a calculator to add or subtract.

15.
```
  391
+ 207
```

16.
```
  689
− 319
```

17.
```
  312
+ 149
```

18.
```
  723
− 119
```

19.
```
  342
+  87
```

Subtracting with Regrouping Hundreds

Find the difference. Regroup hundreds if you need to.

1.

Subtract the ones.	Regroup.	Subtract the tens.	Subtract the hundreds.

H	T	O
3	2	9
− 1	4	6

H	T	O
²3̶	¹²2̶	9
− 1	4	6

H	T	O
²3̶	¹²2̶	9
− 1	4	6

H	T	O
²3̶	¹²2̶	9
− 1	4	6

2. 668
− 391

3. 449
− 86

4. 833
− 172

5. 551
− 470

6. 306
− 152

7. 976
− 215

8. 360
− 280

9. 648
− 162

10. 739
− 524

11. 989
− 197

MIXED APPLICATIONS

12. The Smiths have traveled 284 miles out of a 615-mile trip. How many more miles will they travel?

_____

13. The Jacksons traveled 487 miles to visit an aunt. Then they traveled 225 miles more to visit Grandmother. How far had they traveled then?

_____

WRITER'S CORNER

14. Use the facts to write an estimation problem.

_____

_____

_____

Dallas to St. Louis: 630 miles
Dallas to Tulsa: 257 miles
St. Louis to Denver: 852 miles

Regroup Tens and Hundreds

Sometimes you need to regroup more than once. Sometimes you do not need to regroup. Find the difference. Regroup if you need to.

1.   546
   − 459
	2. 949
	   − 368
		3. 815
		   − 438
			4. 746
			   − 209
				5. 912
				   − 798

6.   869
   − 679
	7. 452
	   − 317
		8. 546
		   − 281
			9. 515
			   − 495
				10. 728
				   − 384

11. $219 - 68 =$ _____   12. $489 - 392 =$ _____

MIXED APPLICATIONS

13. In June, Hank jogged 181 miles and Marcie jogged 214 miles. How many more miles did Marcie jog than Hank?

_____

14. Marcie jogged 214 miles in June, 197 miles in July, and 84 miles in August. How many miles did she jog in the 3-month period?

_____

NUMBER SENSE

15. Complete the numbers to form two 3-digit odd numbers and two 3-digit even numbers.

7 __ __   2 __ __   3 __ __   6 __ __
odd   odd   even   even

Use the numbers you wrote to solve. Write *odd* or *even* beside the difference.

even 6 __ __ − even − 3 __ __	even 6 __ __ − odd − 2 __ __	odd 7 __ __ − odd − 2 __ __	odd 7 __ __ − even − 3 __ __

Exploring Subtraction with Zeros

Use place-value models. Regroup to solve each problem.
Circle *a*, *b*, or *c* to show how you regrouped.

1. 503
    − 258

    a.
H	T	O
4	10	13

    b.
H	T	O
4	9	13

    c.
H	T	O
3	9	10

2. 800
    − 349

    a.
H	T	O
7	10	10

    b.
H	T	O
7	9	10

    c.
H	T	O
8	9	10

3. 602
    − 498

    a.
H	T	O
5	10	12

    b.
H	T	O
6	9	12

    c.
H	T	O
5	9	12

4. 960
    − 386

    a.
H	T	O
8	15	10

    b.
H	T	O
8	15	0

    c.
H	T	O
8	16	10

5. 610
    − 492

    a.
H	T	O
6	9	10

    b.
H	T	O
5	9	10

    c.
H	T	O
5	10	10

MIXED REVIEW

Add.

6. 9
    6
    + 8

7. 27
    15
    + 15

8. 32
    18
    + 10

9. 50
    50
    + 14

10. 371
    200
    + 63

Subtracting Across Zeros

Find the difference.

1.	508	2.	900	3.	807	4.	800	5.	609
	− 412		− 376		− 295		− 478		− 597

6.	501	7.	203	8.	904	9.	703	10.	600
	− 347		− 95		− 369		− 285		− 401

Use mental math to solve each problem.

11. $800 - 300 =$ _____

12. $700 -$ _____ $= 300$

13. $900 -$ _____ $= 700$

14. $600 - 400 =$ _____

MIXED APPLICATIONS

15. A sports car can go 192 kilometers per hour, but the top speed allowed on some highways is 88 kilometers per hour. How many more kilometers per hour can the car travel than it is allowed to?

_____

16. The total distance of a car race is 800 kilometers. If a car racer has traveled 489 kilometers, how many more kilometers must he drive to complete the race?

_____

VISUAL THINKING

17. Draw a picture to show how you would use place-value models to solve the problem $703 - 289$. Then solve.

$703 - 289$

_____

Using Addition to Check Subtraction

Find the difference. Check by adding. Show your work.

1. 861   _____
    − 644 + _____
          _____

2. 853   _____
    − 427 + _____
          _____

3. 590   _____
    − 46 + _____
          _____

4. 748   _____
    − 145 + _____
          _____

5. 966   _____
    − 419 + _____
          _____

6. 608   _____
    − 348 + _____
          _____

7. 476   _____
    − 207 + _____
          _____

8. 819   _____
    − 425 + _____
          _____

MIXED APPLICATIONS

9. A taxi driver travels 465 miles in Week 1 and 582 miles in Week 2. How many more miles does he drive in Week 2?

    _____

10. There were 267 people at one concert and 405 people at another concert. How many people were at the concerts?

    _____

LOGICAL REASONING

11. Look at the fact family on the left. Then use reasoning to complete the addition and subtraction sentences on the right.

Fact Family
4 + 7 = 11
7 + 4 = 11
11 − 4 = 7
11 − 7 = 4

    If 273 + 568 = 841, then

    568 + 273 = _____,

    841 − 273 = _____,

    and 841 − 568 = _____.

Exploring Using a Clock

Write the time for each clock face.

1.

_____

2.

_____

3.

_____

Begin at the 12. Write how many minutes the minute hand has moved. Count by fives. Use your clock face.

4.

_____

5.

_____

6.

_____

MIXED APPLICATIONS

7. When Fay's mother asked what time it was, Fay told her that the minute hand was on the 12 and the hour hand was on the 3. What time was it?

_____

8. The minute hand on Fay's clock was on the 8. Fay's mother said they would leave for the park in 5 minutes. Where will the minute hand be then?

_____

MIXED REVIEW

Find the sum or difference.

9.	**10.**	**11.**	**12.**	**13.**
590	801	434	980	700
+ 242	− 275	− 93	+ 78	− 186

20

Time After the Hour

Use your clock face.

A.

B.

C.

	Clock A	Clock B	Clock C
1. Write the time shown on each clock.	_____	_____	_____
2. Write the time 1 hour later than shown.	_____	_____	_____
3. Write the time 30 minutes later than shown.	_____	_____	_____
4. Write the time 15 minutes later than shown.	_____	_____	_____

MIXED APPLICATIONS

Use your clock face. Solve.

5. Nathan's party began at 2:30. It lasted for 1 hour. At what time was the party over?

_____

6. The children started playing games at 2:45. They played for 30 minutes. At what time did they stop playing?

_____

EVERYDAY MATH CONNECTION

Write the time as you would see it on a digital clock.
Then write the words that tell the time.

7.
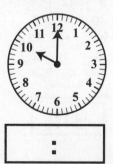

┌─────────┐
│   :   │
└─────────┘

_____

8.
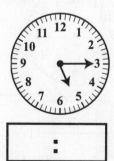

┌─────────┐
│   :   │
└─────────┘

_____

9.

┌─────────┐
│   :   │
└─────────┘

_____

Name _____ Date _____

Exploring Time to the Minute

Count by fives to show the minutes that have passed from the first clock to the second clock.

1.

5, _____, _____, _____

2.

5, _____, _____, _____, _____

3.

5, _____, _____, _____

4.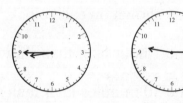

5, _____, _____, _____, _____

Write the time 9 minutes later.

5.

_____

6.

_____

7.

_____

VISUAL THINKING

Draw the hands on each analog clock to match the time shown on the digital clock.

8.

`4:25`

9.

`1:55`

10.

`9:11`

Unit 4
Core Skills Math, Grade 3

Use Data

This is Paul's schedule for one day at camp. Read the schedule. Write the answers.

9:00–9:30	9:30–10:30	10:30–12:30	12:30–1:00	1:00–1:30	1:30–2:00	2:00–3:00
Breakfast	Music	Hiking	Lunch	Crafts	Sailing	Swimming

1. When does hiking begin?

_____

2. When does hiking end?

_____

3. How long is hiking?

_____

4. How long is swimming?

_____

5. How long is sailing?

_____

6. How long is music?

_____

7. How many minutes pass from the beginning of breakfast until the beginning of music?

_____

8. Which eating time is longer? Write *breakfast*, *lunch*, or *same length*.

_____

NUMBER SENSE

Circle the better estimate.

9. Paul swims from 2:00 to 3:15.

He swims for about _____.   a half hour   an hour

Minutes

Write the times.

1.

_____:_____ _____:_____ _____:_____ _____:_____

2.

_____:_____ _____:_____ _____:_____ _____:_____

3.

_____:_____ _____:_____ _____:_____ _____:_____

NUMBER SENSE

Circle the better answer.

4. Dee jogs until 4:20.
It is almost _____.

4:00   4:30

5. Angie swims until 4:55.
It is almost _____.

4:30   5:00

Telling Time

Write the time in numbers and in words.

1.

_____

_____

_____

2.

_____

_____

_____

3.

_____

_____

_____

Match the time with the clock.

4. four minutes past six

5. twenty-three minutes to eight

$$7:37$$

$$6:04$$

MIXED APPLICATIONS

6. Suki spent 14 minutes mixing the muffin batter. She baked the muffins 22 minutes. How many minutes did it take to make the muffins?

_____

7. Jim turned on the oven at 3:00. Jason made bread dough at 2:50. Helen put rolls in the oven at a quarter past three. Which one happened first?

_____

LOGICAL REASONING

Circle the time that fits both clues.

8. The time is given in quarter hours. It is earlier than half past six.

four-ten   five-fifteen   six forty-five

Time: A.M. and P.M.

Write the time by using numbers and A.M. or P.M.

1. The sun rises.

_____

2. The gas station closes.

_____

3. Maria eats lunch.

_____

4. the time you start school

_____

5. the time you eat dinner

_____

MIXED APPLICATIONS

6. A movie on whales was shown at noon. A movie on dolphins was shown at two-twenty. Which movie came first?

_____

7. The class saw a film about sharks. It started at fifteen minutes before eleven. Write the time using A.M. or P.M.

_____

EVERYDAY MATH CONNECTION

The time card shows the hours that Roberto worked for three days. Use the time card to answer the questions.

8. When did Roberto leave work for the day on Wednesday?

_____

9. When did Roberto return to work from lunch on Tuesday?

_____

Time Card				
Name: Roberto				
	In	Out	In	Out
Mon	8:30	11:30	12:30	4:30
Tue	9:00	12:00	1:00	5:00
Wed	8:00	11:00	1:00	6:00

Exploring Multiplication with 2 and 5

Circle groups of 2 shoes. Complete the sentences to find out how many shoes there are.

1.

2 + 2 + 2 = _____

3 equal groups of 2 = _____

3 × 2 = _____

2.

2 + 2 + 2 + 2 = _____

4 equal groups of 2 = _____

_____ × 2 = _____

3.

2 + 2 = _____

2 equal groups of 2 = _____

_____ × 2 = _____

4.

2 + 2 + 2 + 2 + 2 = _____

5 equal groups of 2 = _____

_____ × 2 = _____

MIXED APPLICATIONS

Use cubes. Write a number sentence to solve.

5. There were 5 jugglers in the circus. Each juggler had 5 balls. How many balls were there?

_____ × _____ = _____

_____ balls

6. There were 5 circus wagons. In each wagon there were 3 circus dogs. How many dogs were there?

_____ × _____ = _____

_____ dogs

LOGICAL REASONING

7. How is counting your pairs of socks similar to multiplication by 2? Write a sentence to explain.

_____

Multiplying with 3 and 4

Use punch-out dollars. Complete the multiplication sentences.

1.

Circle groups of 3.

_____ × \$3 = \$_____

2.

Circle groups of 4.

_____ × \$4 = \$_____

3.

Circle groups of 4.

_____ × \$4 = \$_____

4.

Circle groups of 3.

_____ × \$3 = \$_____

MIXED APPLICATIONS

5. Casey has 2 groups of \$4. Colton has 3 groups of \$3. Who has more dollars?

_____

6. Sasha has 4 groups of \$3. Amber has 5 groups of \$2. Who has more dollars?

_____

VISUAL THINKING

Circle the answer.

7. Which stacks would be higher: 4 stacks of 5 umbrellas, or 5 stacks of 4 umbrellas?

4 stacks of 5 umbrellas   5 stacks of 4 umbrellas

28

Name _____ Date _____

Vertical Multiplication

Use cubes. Write the multiplication fact both ways.

1.

$$\times \underline{\hspace{2cm}}$$

$$\underline{\hspace{1.5cm}} \times \underline{\hspace{1.5cm}} = \underline{\hspace{1.5cm}}$$

2.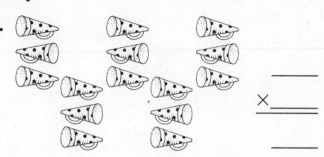

$$\times \underline{\hspace{2cm}}$$

$$\underline{\hspace{1.5cm}} \times \underline{\hspace{1.5cm}} = \underline{\hspace{1.5cm}}$$

3.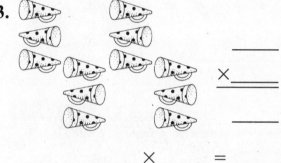

$$\times \underline{\hspace{2cm}}$$

$$\underline{\hspace{1.5cm}} \times \underline{\hspace{1.5cm}} = \underline{\hspace{1.5cm}}$$

4.

$$\times \underline{\hspace{2cm}}$$

$$\underline{\hspace{1.5cm}} \times \underline{\hspace{1.5cm}} = \underline{\hspace{1.5cm}}$$

5.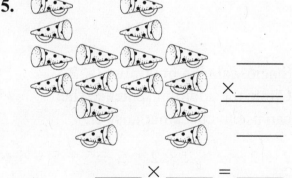

$$\times \underline{\hspace{2cm}}$$

$$\underline{\hspace{1.5cm}} \times \underline{\hspace{1.5cm}} = \underline{\hspace{1.5cm}}$$

6.

$$\times \underline{\hspace{2cm}}$$

$$\underline{\hspace{1.5cm}} \times \underline{\hspace{1.5cm}} = \underline{\hspace{1.5cm}}$$

WRITER'S CORNER

7. Make up a clown story about any multiplication fact. Tell your story to a friend. Write the fact two ways.

$$\times \underline{\hspace{2cm}}$$

$$\underline{\hspace{1.5cm}} \times \underline{\hspace{1.5cm}} = \underline{\hspace{1.5cm}}$$

Multiplication in Any Order

Write the number sentence.

1.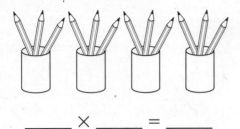

_____ × _____ = _____

2.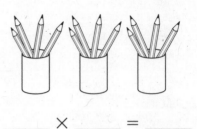

_____ × _____ = _____

3.

_____ × _____ = _____

4.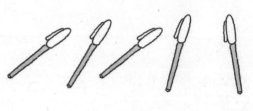

_____ × _____ = _____

5.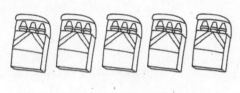

_____ × _____ = _____

6.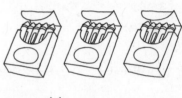

_____ × _____ = _____

MIXED APPLICATIONS

7. Hector wants to multiply 3 × 4. Circle the addition sentence he can use to check his answer.

   3 + 3 + 3   4 + 4 + 4

8. Stacie wants to multiply 5 × 2. Circle the addition sentence she can use to check her answer.

   2 + 2 + 2 + 2 + 2   5 + 5 + 5 + 5 + 5

STORY CORNER

9. Write a story about the picture. Then write the number sentence.

_____

_____

_____ × _____ = _____

30

Multiplying with a Calculator

Use a calculator for skip-counting and multiplying.

1. Alicia has 4 clown hats. Each hat has 3 feathers. How many feathers are there in all?

$$3 + 3 + 3 + 3 = \underline{\hspace{1cm}}$$

$$4 \times 3 = \underline{\hspace{1cm}}$$

2. There are 3 circus rings. There are 3 elephants in each ring. How many elephants are in the rings?

$$3 + 3 + 3 = \underline{\hspace{1cm}}$$

$$3 \times 3 = \underline{\hspace{1cm}}$$

3. There are 5 horses. There are 2 riders on each horse. How many riders are there?

$$2 + 2 + 2 + 2 + 2 = \underline{\hspace{1cm}}$$

$$5 \times 2 = \underline{\hspace{1cm}}$$

4. Tran bought 4 tickets. Each ticket cost $5. How much did he spend?

$$\$5 + \$5 + \$5 + \$5 = \$\underline{\hspace{1cm}}$$

$$4 \times \$5 = \$\underline{\hspace{1cm}}$$

5. A juice drink cost $2. Jill bought 3 of them. How much did she spend?

$$\$2 + \$2 + \$2 = \$\underline{\hspace{1cm}}$$

$$3 \times \$2 = \$\underline{\hspace{1cm}}$$

6. Each clown car has 4 wheels. How many wheels are there on 4 clown cars?

$$4 + 4 + 4 + 4 = \underline{\hspace{1cm}}$$

$$4 \times 4 = \underline{\hspace{1cm}}$$

PROBLEM SOLVING

Write a number sentence. Solve.

7. The circus was in town for 2 weeks. There were 4 shows each week. How many shows were there in all?

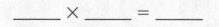

$$\underline{\hspace{1cm}} \times \underline{\hspace{1cm}} = \underline{\hspace{1cm}}$$

8. There are 4 circus tents with 1 clown in each. How many clowns are there?

$$\underline{\hspace{1cm}} \times \underline{\hspace{1cm}} = \underline{\hspace{1cm}}$$

Connecting Addition and Multiplication

Write the addition sentence and the multiplication sentence for each picture.

1.

_____

2.

_____

Draw a picture for each multiplication sentence.

3. $4 \times 4 = 16$

4. $3 \times 3 = 9$

5. $5 \times 5 = 25$

MIXED APPLICATIONS

Use counters. Solve.

6. Pete lines up his model airplanes in 5 rows. Each row has 3 airplanes. How many airplanes does Pete have?

_____

7. Each of 4 boys bought a 4-pack of mini-cars. Write an addition sentence and a multiplication sentence to show how many mini-cars they bought.

_____

EVERYDAY MATH CONNECTION

A nickel is worth 5¢. The value of a group of nickels can be found by adding or multiplying. Write an addition sentence and a multiplication sentence to tell the value of each group of nickels.

8.

_____

9.

_____

Multiply Using 2 as a Factor

Complete the multiplication sentence for each picture.

1.

$5 \times 2 = \underline{\hspace{1cm}}$

2.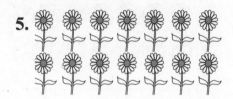

$6 \times 2 = \underline{\hspace{1cm}}$

3.

$2 \times 8 = \underline{\hspace{1cm}}$

Write the multiplication sentence for each picture.

4.

$\underline{\hspace{4cm}}$

5.

$\underline{\hspace{4cm}}$

6.

$\underline{\hspace{4cm}}$

Find the product. You many draw a picture or use a number line.

7.	**8.**	**9.**	**10.**	**11.**	**12.**
$\begin{array}{r} 2 \\ \times 5 \\ \hline \end{array}$	$\begin{array}{r} 9 \\ \times 2 \\ \hline \end{array}$	$\begin{array}{r} 4 \\ \times 2 \\ \hline \end{array}$	$\begin{array}{r} 7 \\ \times 2 \\ \hline \end{array}$	$\begin{array}{r} 2 \\ \times 8 \\ \hline \end{array}$	$\begin{array}{r} 2 \\ \times 6 \\ \hline \end{array}$

MIXED APPLICATIONS

Write a number sentence. Solve.

13. Sal has 6 rosebushes. He picks 2 roses from each bush. How many roses does he pick?

$\underline{\hspace{5cm}}$

14. Sal buys 24 pansies, 36 begonias, and 48 violas. How many flowers does Sal buy?

$\underline{\hspace{5cm}}$

LOGICAL REASONING

15. Luci, Juana, and Marco collect postcards when they go on trips. Luci has 3 fewer postcards than Juana. Marco has collected 5 postcards on each of 2 different trips. Juana has 2 times as many postcards as Marco. How many postcards does each person have?

$\underline{\hspace{12cm}}$

Unit 5
Core Skills Math, Grade 3

Multiply Using 3 as a Factor

Use the number line to find the product.

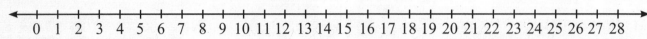

1. $3 \times 8 =$ _____   **2.** $4 \times 3 =$ _____   **3.** $3 \times 6 =$ _____

Write the multiplication sentence for each picture.

4.

_____

5.

_____

6.

_____

Find the product.

7.	**8.**	**9.**	**10.**	**11.**	**12.**
2	9	3	7	3	3
$\times 3$	$\times 3$	$\times 8$	$\times 3$	$\times 5$	$\times 6$

MIXED APPLICATIONS

13. There are 5 shelves of footballs in a closet. Each shelf has 3 footballs. How many footballs are there?

_____

14. Kiri hunts lost golf balls. She finds 16 balls near the clubhouse. She finds 6 in one sand trap, 9 in another trap, and 10 in the bushes. How many golf balls does she find?

_____

VISUAL THINKING

Draw number lines to help you solve.

15. José and Edward each filled a photo album. Edward said he had more photos than José because his album had 4 pages more than José's. José said he had more photos because he put 6 photos on each of the 5 pages in his album and Edward put 4 on each page. Which boy was right? How many photos did each boy have?

_____

Name _____ Date _____

Multiply Using 4 as a Factor

Draw a picture for each multiplication sentence. Solve.

1. $8 \times 4 =$ _____

2. $2 \times 4 =$ _____

3. $7 \times 4 =$ _____

Find the product.

4.	5.	6.	7.	8.	9.
$\begin{array}{r} 8 \\ \times\,3 \\ \hline \end{array}$	$\begin{array}{r} 3 \\ \times\,9 \\ \hline \end{array}$	$\begin{array}{r} 4 \\ \times\,2 \\ \hline \end{array}$	$\begin{array}{r} 7 \\ \times\,4 \\ \hline \end{array}$	$\begin{array}{r} 4 \\ \times\,9 \\ \hline \end{array}$	$\begin{array}{r} 3 \\ \times\,7 \\ \hline \end{array}$

10. $3 \times 3 =$ _____

11. $4 \times 6 =$ _____

12. $4 \times 4 =$ _____

13. $4 \times 5 =$ _____

MIXED APPLICATIONS

14. Mabel buys 6 cards with animal buttons on them. Each card has 4 buttons. How many animal buttons does Mabel buy?

_____

15. Jen sews animal buttons on her clothes. She puts 4 tigers on her shirt, 3 giraffes on her hat, 16 seals on her skirt, and 1 lion on each glove. How many animal buttons does she sew?

_____

EVERYDAY MATH CONNECTION

Four quarters equal one dollar. Write how many quarters equal each group of dollars.

    =

16. $2 =$ _____ quarters

17. $3 =$ _____ quarters

18. $4 =$ _____ quarters

35

Multiply Using 5 as a Factor

Draw a picture for each multiplication sentence. Solve.

1. $4 \times 5 =$ _____ **2.** $3 \times 5 =$ _____ **3.** $6 \times 5 =$ _____

Find the product.

4. $8 \times 5 =$ _____ **5.** $2 \times 5 =$ _____ **6.** $7 \times 5 =$ _____ **7.** $5 \times 5 =$ _____

8.   5   **9.**   7   **10.**   5   **11.**   8   **12.**   9   **13.**   4
    $\times 9$ $\times 4$ $\times 1$ $\times 3$ $\times 4$ $\times 5$

Write +, −, or × for each ◯.

14. $5 \bigcirc 3 = 8$ **15.** $5 \bigcirc 3 = 15$ **16.** $5 \bigcirc 3 = 2$

MIXED APPLICATIONS

17. Jiro needs 5 nickels to pay for a pack of baseball cards. Write a multiplication sentence to find the cost.

_____

18. Milo gave the clerk a $1 bill. The clerk gave Milo 4 dimes in change. How much change did Milo get? How much was his purchase?

_____

NUMBER SENSE

Solve the number puzzles.

19. I am a factor of 30. The other factor is 5. What number am I?

_____

20. I am a factor of 25. When I am multiplied by myself, the product is 25. What number am I?

_____

    Core Skills Math, Grade 3

Multiply Using 1 and 0 as Factors

Find the product.

1. $9 \times 0 =$ _____

2. $8 \times 1 =$ _____

3. $4 \times 0 =$ _____

4. $7 \times 1 =$ _____

5. $6 \times 0 =$ _____

6. $3 \times 1 =$ _____

7. $9 \times 1 =$ _____

8. $10 \times 0 =$ _____

9. $8 \times 0 =$ _____

10. $10 \times 1 =$ _____

11. $7 \times 0 =$ _____

12. $6 \times 1 =$ _____

13.
$$\begin{array}{r} 4 \\ \times\, 0 \\ \hline \end{array}$$

14.
$$\begin{array}{r} 3 \\ \times\, 1 \\ \hline \end{array}$$

15.
$$\begin{array}{r} 2 \\ \times\, 0 \\ \hline \end{array}$$

16.
$$\begin{array}{r} 9 \\ \times\, 0 \\ \hline \end{array}$$

17.
$$\begin{array}{r} 1 \\ \times\, 1 \\ \hline \end{array}$$

18.
$$\begin{array}{r} 0 \\ \times\, 8 \\ \hline \end{array}$$

19.
$$\begin{array}{r} 5 \\ \times\, 1 \\ \hline \end{array}$$

20.
$$\begin{array}{r} 3 \\ \times\, 0 \\ \hline \end{array}$$

21.
$$\begin{array}{r} 4 \\ \times\, 1 \\ \hline \end{array}$$

22.
$$\begin{array}{r} 2 \\ \times\, 0 \\ \hline \end{array}$$

23.
$$\begin{array}{r} 0 \\ \times\, 5 \\ \hline \end{array}$$

24.
$$\begin{array}{r} 1 \\ \times\, 2 \\ \hline \end{array}$$

MIXED APPLICATIONS

25. Marie put 1 sticker on each page of her 8-page sticker album. How many stickers did Marie put in her album?

_____

26. Inez has 37 fuzzy stickers and 61 scented stickers. How many more scented stickers than fuzzy stickers does Inez have?

_____

MIXED REVIEW

Find the sum or difference.

27.
$$\begin{array}{r} 872 \\ -\, 381 \\ \hline \end{array}$$

28.
$$\begin{array}{r} 565 \\ -\, 228 \\ \hline \end{array}$$

29.
$$\begin{array}{r} 476 \\ +\, 316 \\ \hline \end{array}$$

30.
$$\begin{array}{r} 903 \\ -\, 177 \\ \hline \end{array}$$

31.
$$\begin{array}{r} 396 \\ +\, 505 \\ \hline \end{array}$$

Name _____ Date _____

Exploring Arrays

Write the multiplication sentence for each array.

1.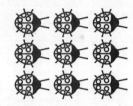

_____

2.

_____

3.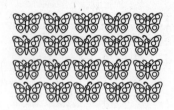

_____

4.

_____

5.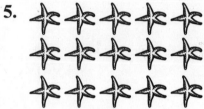

_____

6.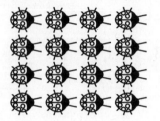

_____

7. Look at your answers to Exercises 1–6. Write the multiplication sentences with products that are square numbers.

_____

Find the product. Write *yes* or *no* to tell which products are square numbers.

8.	9.	10.	11.	12.	13.
5	3	2	6	1	1
× 5	× 8	× 2	× 5	× 8	× 1
____	____	____	____	____	____

MIXED REVIEW

Find the sum or difference.

14. 396	15. 279	16. 985	17. 918	18. 590
+ 197	− 83	− 230	− 468	+ 179

Find the sum. Write the matching multiplication sentence.

19. 2 + 2 + 2 + 2 = _____   20. 5 + 5 + 5 + 5 + 5 = _____

_____   _____

38

© Houghton Mifflin Harcourt Publishing Company

Unit 5
Core Skills Math, Grade 3

Multiply Using 6 as a Factor

Find the product. If needed, draw an array or picture to help you.

1. $9 \times 6 =$ _____

2. $8 \times 6 =$ _____

3. $6 \times 5 =$ _____

4. $7 \times 6 =$ _____

Find the product.

5.
$$
\begin{array}{r}
3 \\
\times\, 6 \\
\hline
\end{array}
$$

6.
$$
\begin{array}{r}
4 \\
\times\, 6 \\
\hline
\end{array}
$$

7.
$$
\begin{array}{r}
6 \\
\times\, 6 \\
\hline
\end{array}
$$

8.
$$
\begin{array}{r}
6 \\
\times\, 8 \\
\hline
\end{array}
$$

9.
$$
\begin{array}{r}
6 \\
\times\, 5 \\
\hline
\end{array}
$$

10.
$$
\begin{array}{r}
1 \\
\times\, 6 \\
\hline
\end{array}
$$

11.
$$
\begin{array}{r}
4 \\
\times\, 8 \\
\hline
\end{array}
$$

12.
$$
\begin{array}{r}
5 \\
\times\, 6 \\
\hline
\end{array}
$$

13.
$$
\begin{array}{r}
2 \\
\times\, 6 \\
\hline
\end{array}
$$

14.
$$
\begin{array}{r}
5 \\
\times\, 7 \\
\hline
\end{array}
$$

15.
$$
\begin{array}{r}
6 \\
\times\, 7 \\
\hline
\end{array}
$$

16.
$$
\begin{array}{r}
6 \\
\times\, 9 \\
\hline
\end{array}
$$

MIXED APPLICATIONS

Solve.

17. There are 8 DVDs on each of 6 shelves. How many DVDs are on the shelves?

_____

18. Mary buys 6 CDs at $2 each and a case for $5. How much money does she spend?

_____

NUMBER SENSE

19. One factor is 5. The product is 35. What is the other factor?

_____

20. The product is 36. Both factors are the same. What are the factors?

_____

Multiply Using 7 as a Factor

Use what you know about the Order Property to find the product.

1. $7 \times 9 = $ _____　　**2.** $7 \times 3 = $ _____　　**3.** $7 \times 2 = $ _____　　**4.** $8 \times 7 = $ _____

5. $7 \times 6 = $ _____　　**6.** $9 \times 7 = $ _____　　**7.** $5 \times 7 = $ _____　　**8.** $7 \times 4 = $ _____

Find the product.

9.　　8　　**10.**　　1　　**11.**　　2　　**12.**　　9　　**13.**　　2　　**14.**　　4
$\times 7$　　　　$\times 7$　　　　$\times 7$　　　　$\times 3$　　　　$\times 8$　　　　$\times 6$

15.　　4　　**16.**　　7　　**17.**　　6　　**18.**　　8　　**19.**　　7　　**20.**　　7
$\times 9$　　　　$\times 5$　　　　$\times 3$　　　　$\times 6$　　　　$\times 7$　　　　$\times 8$

MIXED APPLICATIONS

Solve.

21. Risa buys a model for $7, paint for $2, and glue for $1. How much does Risa spend?

_____

22. Thuy puts 7 toy boats in each of 8 rows. How many boats does he have?

_____

EVERYDAY MATH CONNECTION

23. There are 7 days in 1 week. A month is just over 4 weeks long. How many days is that?

_____

24. A year is about 52 weeks long. How many days is that? Use your calculator to help you.

_____

40

Multiply Using 8 as a Factor

Complete the table. Find the product.

1.

×	0	1	2	3	4	5	6	7	8	9
8										

Find the product.

2.	8	3.	4	4.	8	5.	5	6.	9	7.	8
	× 7		× 9		× 8		× 8		× 7		× 2

8. $8 \times 3 =$ _____ **9.** $9 \times 8 =$ _____ **10.** $4 \times 8 =$ _____ **11.** $6 \times 8 =$ _____

MIXED APPLICATIONS

Solve.

12. Ellen buys toy rings at 8 for $1. She spends $3. How many toy rings does she buy?

13. A plastic model costs $4. A metal model costs $7. How much more does a metal model cost than a plastic model?

_____   _____

EVERYDAY MATH CONNECTION

The standard height of a 1-story room is 8 feet. A building that is 3 stories high may be about 24 feet tall, because $3 \times 8 = 24$.

Find about how tall each of these buildings is.
Use your calculator when needed.

14. 5-story house = about _____ feet tall

15. 8-story apartment house = about _____ feet tall

16. 10-story hotel = about _____ feet tall.

17. 25-story skyscraper = about _____ feet tall

Multiply Using 9 as a Factor

Find the product.

1. $9 \times 3 =$ _____
2. $4 \times 9 =$ _____
3. $9 \times 1 =$ _____
4. $2 \times 9 =$ _____

5. $9 \times 7 =$ _____
6. $9 \times 9 =$ _____
7. $9 \times 5 =$ _____
8. $9 \times 8 =$ _____

Find the product.

9. $\begin{array}{r} 9 \\ \times\, 8 \\ \hline \end{array}$
10. $\begin{array}{r} 7 \\ \times\, 9 \\ \hline \end{array}$
11. $\begin{array}{r} 9 \\ \times\, 4 \\ \hline \end{array}$
12. $\begin{array}{r} 9 \\ \times\, 6 \\ \hline \end{array}$
13. $\begin{array}{r} 9 \\ \times\, 0 \\ \hline \end{array}$
14. $\begin{array}{r} 5 \\ \times\, 9 \\ \hline \end{array}$

15. $\begin{array}{r} 4 \\ \times\, 7 \\ \hline \end{array}$
16. $\begin{array}{r} 6 \\ \times\, 6 \\ \hline \end{array}$
17. $\begin{array}{r} 6 \\ \times\, 8 \\ \hline \end{array}$
18. $\begin{array}{r} 4 \\ \times\, 9 \\ \hline \end{array}$
19. $\begin{array}{r} 9 \\ \times\, 2 \\ \hline \end{array}$
20. $\begin{array}{r} 3 \\ \times\, 9 \\ \hline \end{array}$

MIXED APPLICATIONS

Solve.

21. Mr. Eaton is 38 years old. Maria is 29 years younger than Mr. Eaton. How old is Maria?

_____

22. A year in a human's life is said to equal 7 years in a dog's life. If a dog is 9 human-years old, what is its age in dog-years?

_____

NUMBER SENSE

Fill in the numbers to make each fact true.

23. $10 \times 1 = 10$

$9 \times 1 =$ _____ less than 10

$10 - 1 =$ _____ , so $9 \times 1 =$ _____

24. $10 \times 2 = 20$

$9 \times 2 =$ _____ less than 20

$20 - 2 =$ _____ , so $9 \times 2 =$ _____

25. $10 \times 3 = 30$

$9 \times 3 =$ _____ less than 30

$30 - 3 =$ _____ , so $9 \times 3 =$ _____

26. $10 \times 4 = 40$

$9 \times 4 =$ _____ less than 40

$40 - 4 =$ _____ , so $9 \times 4 =$ _____

The Multiplication Facts

Find the product.

1.	2.	3.	4.	5.	6.
3 × 8	6 × 9	2 × 4	4 × 6	8 × 0	1 × 9

7.	8.	9.	10.	11.	12.
6 × 8	9 × 9	5 × 4	3 × 6	5 × 0	8 × 9

13.	14.	15.	16.	17.	18.
1 × 7	7 × 6	0 × 2	4 × 9	7 × 7	2 × 9

MIXED APPLICATIONS

Solve.

19. Eric buys 3 balloons for $2 each and 4 balloons for $3 each. How much does Eric spend?

_____

20. Anya buys 37 balloons for a party. She gives each guest 5 balloons. She has 2 balloons left. How many guests are at the party?

_____

VISUAL THINKING

Write 2 multiplication facts for each picture.

21. _____ × _____ = _____

_____ × _____ = _____

22. _____ × _____ = _____

_____ × _____ = _____

Name _____ Date _____

Model with Arrays

Write a multiplication sentence for the array.

1.

$3 \times 7 =$ _____

2.

$2 \times 5 =$ _____

Draw an array to find the product.

3. $4 \times 2 =$ _____

4. $4 \times 4 =$ _____

5. $3 \times 2 =$ _____

6. $2 \times 8 =$ _____

PROBLEM SOLVING

7. Lenny is moving tables in the school cafeteria. He places all the tables in a 7×4 array. How many tables are in the cafeteria?

_____

8. Ms. DiMeo directs the school choir. She has the singers stand in 3 rows. There are 8 singers in each row. How many singers are there in all?

_____

44

Name _____   Date _____

Multiply with 2 and 4

Write a multiplication sentence for the model.

1.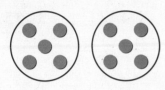

    Think: There are 2 groups of
    5 counters.

    _____ × _____ = _____

2.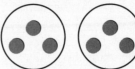

    _____ × _____ = _____

Find the product.

3.   2
   × 6

4.   4
   × 8

5.   2
   × 3

6.   4
   × 6

7.   4
   × 4

8.   2
   × 7

9.   4
   × 5

10.   2
   × 4

PROBLEM SOLVING

11. On Monday, Steven read 9 pages of his new book. To finish the first chapter on Tuesday, he needs to read double the number of pages he read on Monday. How many pages does he need to read on Tuesday?

    _____

12. Courtney's school is having a family game night. Each table has 4 players. There are 7 tables in all. How many players are at the game night?

    _____

45

Multiply with 3 and 6

Find the product.

1. $6 \times 4 = $ _____

Think: You can use doubles.
$3 \times 4 = 12$
$12 + 12 = 24$

2. $3 \times 7 = $ _____

3. _____ $= 2 \times 6$

4. _____ $= 3 \times 5$

5. $1 \times 3 = $ _____

6. _____ $= 6 \times 8$

7. $3 \times 9 = $ _____

8. _____ $= 6 \times 6$

9.
$$\begin{array}{r} 4 \\ \times\, 3 \\ \hline \end{array}$$

10.
$$\begin{array}{r} 6 \\ \times\, 5 \\ \hline \end{array}$$

11.
$$\begin{array}{r} 2 \\ \times\, 3 \\ \hline \end{array}$$

12.
$$\begin{array}{r} 6 \\ \times\, 3 \\ \hline \end{array}$$

13.
$$\begin{array}{r} 10 \\ \times\, 6 \\ \hline \end{array}$$

14.
$$\begin{array}{r} 3 \\ \times\, 6 \\ \hline \end{array}$$

15.
$$\begin{array}{r} 7 \\ \times\, 6 \\ \hline \end{array}$$

16.
$$\begin{array}{r} 3 \\ \times\, 0 \\ \hline \end{array}$$

17.
$$\begin{array}{r} 9 \\ \times\, 6 \\ \hline \end{array}$$

18.
$$\begin{array}{r} 3 \\ \times\, 3 \\ \hline \end{array}$$

19.
$$\begin{array}{r} 10 \\ \times\, 3 \\ \hline \end{array}$$

20.
$$\begin{array}{r} 1 \\ \times\, 6 \\ \hline \end{array}$$

PROBLEM SOLVING

21. James got 3 hits in each of his baseball games. He has played 4 baseball games. How many hits has he had in all?

_____

22. Mrs. Burns is buying muffins. There are 6 muffins in each box. If she buys 5 boxes, how many muffins will she buy?

_____

Patterns on the Multiplication Table

Is the product even or odd? Write *even* or *odd*.

1. 2 × 7 = _____   **Think:** Products   **2.** 4 × 6 = _____   **3.** 8 × 3 = _____
with 2 as a factor
are even.

4. 2 × 3 = _____   **5.** 9 × 9 = _____   **6.** 5 × 7 = _____   **7.** 6 × 3 = _____

Use the multiplication table. Describe a pattern you see.

8. in the column for 5

_____

_____

×	0	1	2	3	4	5	6	7	8	9	10
0	0	0	0	0	0	0	0	0	0	0	0
1	0	1	2	3	4	5	6	7	8	9	10
2	0	2	4	6	8	10	12	14	16	18	20
3	0	3	6	9	12	15	18	21	24	27	30
4	0	4	8	12	16	20	24	28	32	36	40
5	0	5	10	15	20	25	30	35	40	45	50
6	0	6	12	18	24	30	36	42	48	54	60
7	0	7	14	21	28	35	42	49	56	63	70
8	0	8	16	24	32	40	48	56	64	72	80
9	0	9	18	27	36	45	54	63	72	81	90
10	0	10	20	30	40	50	60	70	80	90	100

9. in the row for 10

_____

_____

_____

10. in the rows for 3 and 6

_____

_____

_____

PROBLEM SOLVING

11. Carl shades a row in the multiplication
table. The products in the row are all
even. The ones digits in the products
repeat 0, 4, 8, 2, 6. What row does
Carl shade?

_____

12. Jenna says that no row or column
contains products with only odd
numbers. Do you agree? Explain.

_____

_____

Unit 6
Core Skills Math, Grade 3

Describe Patterns

Describe a pattern for the table. Then complete the table.

1.

Pans	1	2	3	4	5
Muffins	6	12	18		

_____

_____

_____

2.

Wagons	2	3	4	5	6
Wheels	8	12	16		

_____

_____

_____

3.

Vases	Flowers
2	14
3	
4	28
5	
6	42

_____

_____

_____

4.

Spiders	Legs
1	8
2	
3	24
4	
5	40

_____

_____

_____

PROBLEM SOLVING

5. Caleb buys 5 cartons of yogurt. Each carton has 8 yogurt cups. How many yogurt cups does Caleb buy?

_____

6. Libby bought 4 packages of pencils. Each package has 6 pencils. How many pencils did Libby buy?

_____

48

Using Multiplication Properties

Write a, b, c, or d to tell which property is shown.

a. Order Property	**b.** Property of One	**c.** Zero Property	**d.** Grouping Property

1. $5 \times 1 = 5$ _____

2. $8 \times 0 = 0$ _____

3. $1 \times 9 = 9 \times 1$ _____

4. $7 \times (3 \times 2) = (7 \times 3) \times 2$ _____

5. $3 \times 4 = 4 \times 3$ _____

Use the multiplication properties to solve.

6. $5 \times 7 = 35$

$7 \times 5 =$ _____

7. $9 \times 4 = 36$

$4 \times 9 =$ _____

8. $6 \times 7 = 42$

$7 \times 6 =$ _____

9. $8 \times 0 =$ _____

10. $1 \times 4 =$ _____

11. $0 \times 7 =$ _____

12. $4 \times (3 \times 2) =$ _____

13. $2 \times (1 \times 9) =$ _____

14. $3 \times (84 \times 0) =$ _____

MIXED APPLICATIONS

15. Beth has 4 boxes of paper clips. She opens the boxes, but they are all empty. Write a number sentence that tells the number of paper clips she has.

_____

16. Beth puts 8 paper clips into each of the 4 boxes. Write a number sentence that tells the number of paper clips in all.

_____

VISUAL THINKING

17. Circle the two arrays that show $3 \times 5 = 5 \times 3$.

   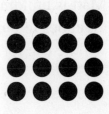

Multiplication Properties

Use multiplication properties to solve.

1. $89 \times 1 =$ _____

2. $148 \times 0 =$ _____

3. $7 \times 15 =$ _____ $\times 7$

4. $(5 \times$ _____$) \times 2 = 5 \times (7 \times 2)$

5. $12{,}876 \times$ _____ $= 12{,}876$

6. $478 \times 0 \times 1 =$ _____

7. $($_____ $\times 4) \times 8 = 16 \times (4 \times 8)$

8. $541 \times 321 =$ _____ $\times 541$

9. $2 \times (50 \times 3) = (2 \times$ _____$) \times 3$

MIXED APPLICATIONS

10. Using 854, write a multiplication sentence that shows the Zero Property.

_____

11. Using 119, write an example of the Property of One.

_____

12. Mary spent $2 a day for lunch, 4 days a week. How much did she spend in 4 weeks?

_____

13. Juan spent $6 on a present. He also bought 3 books at $5 each. How much money did Juan spend?

_____

VISUAL THINKING

14. Matt is building a staircase out of cubes. If he uses 10 cubes to build a 4-step staircase, how many cubes will he use for a 6-step staircase?

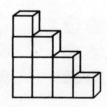

Exploring the Distributive Property

Use the graph paper to find each product.

1. $6 \times 10 =$ _____   **2.** $6 \times 9 =$ _____

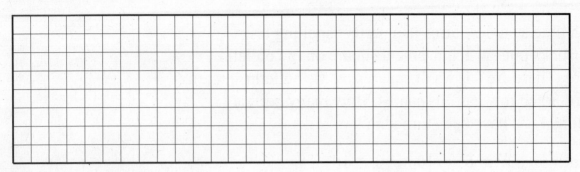

Complete. Find each product.

3. Find 6×19.
$6 \times 10 =$ ___

$6 \times 9 =$ ___

Add.

___ + ___ = ___,

so $6 \times 19 =$ ___

4. Find 3×15.
$3 \times 10 =$ ___

$3 \times 5 =$ ___

Add.

___ + ___ = ___,

so $3 \times 15 =$ ___

5. Find 8×17.
$8 \times 10 =$ ___

$8 \times 7 =$ ___

Add.

___ + ___ = ___,

so $8 \times 17 =$ ___

6. Find 2×12.
$2 \times 10 =$ ___

$2 \times 2 =$ ___

Add.

___ + ___ = ___,

so $2 \times 12 =$ ___

7. Find 9×13.
$9 \times 10 =$ ___

$9 \times 3 =$ ___

Add.

___ + ___ = ___,

so $9 \times 13 =$ ___

8. Find 4×16.
$4 \times 10 =$ ___

$4 \times 6 =$ ___

Add.

___ + ___ = ___,

so $4 \times 16 =$ ___

NUMBER SENSE

9. Write all of the multiplication facts that have a product of 12.

___ $\times$ ___ = 12   ___ $\times$ ___ = 12

___ $\times$ ___ = 12   ___ $\times$ ___ = 12

___ $\times$ ___ = 12   ___ $\times$ ___ = 12

Unit 6
Core Skills Math, Grade 3

Use the Distributive Property

PROBLEM SOLVING

Read each problem and solve.

1. Each time a student turns in a perfect spelling test, Ms. Ricks puts an achievement square on the bulletin board. There are 6 rows of squares on the bulletin board. Each row has 30 squares. How many perfect spelling tests have been turned in?

   Think: $6 \times 30 = 6 \times (10 + 10 + 10)$

   $= 60 + 60 + 60 = 180$

   _____

2. Norma practices violin for 50 minutes every day. How many minutes does Norma practice violin in 7 days?

   _____

3. A kitchen designer is creating a new backsplash for the wall behind a kitchen sink. The backsplash will have 5 rows of tiles. Each row will have 20 tiles. How many tiles are needed for the entire backsplash?

   _____

4. A bowling alley keeps shoes in rows of cubbyholes. There are 9 rows of cubbyholes with 20 cubbyholes in each row. If there is a pair of shoes in every cubbyhole, how many pairs of shoes are there?

   _____

5. The third-grade students are traveling to the science museum in 8 buses. There are 40 students on each bus. How many students are going to the museum?

   _____

Multiplication Strategies with Multiples of 10

Use a number line to find the product.

1. $2 \times 40 =$ _____

2. $4 \times 30 =$ _____

Use place value to find the product.

3. $5 \times 70 = 5 \times$ _____ tens

   $=$ _____ tens $=$ _____

4. $60 \times 4 =$ _____ tens $\times 4$

   $=$ _____ tens $=$ _____

5. $7 \times 30 = 7 \times$ _____ tens

   $=$ _____ tens $=$ _____

6. $90 \times 3 =$ _____ tens $\times 3$

   $=$ _____ tens $=$ _____

PROBLEM SOLVING

7. One exhibit at the aquarium has 5 fish tanks. Each fish tank holds 50 gallons of water. How much water do the 5 tanks hold in all?

   _____

8. In another aquarium display, there are 40 fish in each of 7 large tanks. How many fish are in the display in all?

   _____

53

Multiply Multiples of 10 by 1-Digit Numbers

Find the product. Use base-ten blocks or draw a quick picture.

1. $4 \times 50 =$ _____   **2.** $60 \times 3 =$ _____   **3.** _____ $= 60 \times 5$

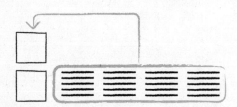

Find the product.

4.   30   **5.**   50   **6.**   60   **7.**   70

     $\times\,8$ $\times\,2$ $\times\,7$ $\times\,4$

8. $6 \times 90 =$ _____   **9.** $9 \times 70 =$ _____   **10.** $8 \times 90 =$ _____   **11.** _____ $= 6 \times 80$

PROBLEM SOLVING

12. Each model car in a set costs $4. There are 30 different model cars in the set. How much would it cost to buy all the model cars in the set?

_____

13. Amanda exercises for 50 minutes each day. How many minutes will she exercise in 7 days?

_____

Exploring Multiplying 2-Digit Numbers

Find the total. Use place-value materials to help you.

1. 4 groups of 15 = _____

2. 3 groups of 24 = _____

3. 3 groups of 16 = _____

4. 2 groups of 37 = _____

Find the product. Use place-value materials to help you.

5. $3 \times 13 =$ _____

6. $5 \times 15 =$ _____

7. $2 \times 28 =$ _____

8. $8 \times 12 =$ _____

9. $4 \times 16 =$ _____

10. $2 \times 43 =$ _____

11. $3 \times 25 =$ _____

12. $4 \times 18 =$ _____

13. two times twenty-nine = _____

14. four times thirty-one = _____

15. The students in each of 4 classes at Andian School recycled 27 foam lunch trays on Monday. How many trays did they recycle on Monday?

_____

16. Foam lunch trays cost the school 2¢ each. How much money do 27 trays cost?

_____

CONSUMER CONNECTION

Some recycling centers pay 5¢ for every aluminum can returned to be recycled. Find the total amount earned by each student.

17. Sierra recycles 34 cans.

She earns _____ ¢.

18. Jamal recycles 28 cans.

He earns _____ ¢.

19. Nina recycles 24 cans.

She earns _____ ¢.

Multiplying 2-Digit Numbers

Find the product. Use place-value materials to help you.

1. 27 $\times$ 2	2. 18 $\times$ 3	3. 42 $\times$ 2	4. 38 $\times$ 2	5. 17 $\times$ 5	6. 19 $\times$ 4

7. 23 $\times$ 4	8. 34 $\times$ 2	9. 16 $\times$ 5	10. 22 $\times$ 4	11. 25 $\times$ 3	12. 18 $\times$ 2

13. $18 \times 4 =$ _____

14. $28 \times 3 =$ _____

15. $13 \times 5 =$ _____

16. $4 \times 13 =$ _____

17. $3 \times 24 =$ _____

18. $5 \times 16 =$ _____

MIXED APPLICATIONS

19. A senator receives 2 letters a day from students. How many letters does the senator receive in a 31-day month?

_____

20. Ms. Dey's class checked the temperature 3 times a day. How many times will they check the temperature in 20 school days?

_____

EVERYDAY MATH CONNECTION

George works at a store. He earns \$9 an hour. Find the amount of money he earns each week.

21. a 35-hour work week

_____

22. a 30-hour work week

_____

23. a 20-hour work week

_____

24. a 45-hour work week

_____

Exploring Division: Sharing

Use counters. Show how many are in each group.

1.

Circle 2 equal groups.
How many are in each group?

_____

2.

Circle 3 equal groups.
How many are in each group?

_____

3.

Circle 3 equal groups.
How many are in each group?

_____

4.

Circle 2 equal groups.
How many are in each group?

_____

VISUAL THINKING

Can you make 2 equal groups? Write *yes* or *no*.

5.

_____

6.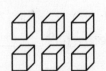

_____

7.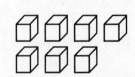

_____

Exploring Division: Separating

Use counters. Show how many groups.

1.

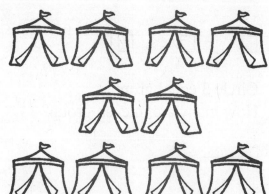

Circle groups of 2.
How many groups? _____

2.

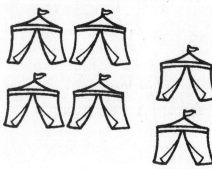

Circle groups of 4.
How many groups? _____

3.

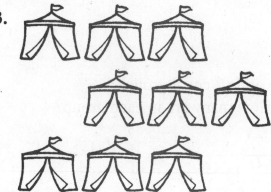

Circle groups of 3.
How many groups? _____

4.

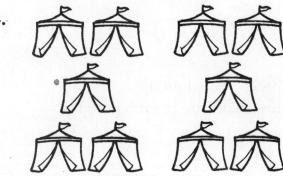

Circle groups of 5.
How many groups? _____

REASONING

5. How many shoes are needed for 4 clowns? _____

6. How many shoes are needed for 5 clowns? _____

Draw a Picture

Draw a picture to solve.

1. There are 9 fish. There are 3 fish in each fishbowl. How many fishbowls are there?

   _____

2. There are 12 pillows. There are 4 pillows on each sofa. How many sofas are there?

   _____

3. There are 15 crayons. There are 3 crayons in each box. How many boxes are there?

   _____

REASONING

Circle the answer. Then draw a picture to check.

4. You have 20 stickers. Which would use more pages?

   putting 4 stickers on each page

   putting 5 stickers on each page

Exploring Division

Answer the questions for each picture.

1.

How many in all? ____

How many rows? ____

How many
in each row? ____

$6 \div 2 =$ ____

2.

How many in all? ____

How many rows? ____

How many
in each row? ____

$21 \div 3 =$ ____

3.

How many in all? ____

How many rows? ____

How many
in each row? ____

$12 \div 3 =$ ____

Divide. Use counters and circles.

4. $15 \div 5 =$ ____   5. $8 \div 4 =$ ____   6. $10 \div 2 =$ ____   7. $28 \div 4 =$ ____

VISUAL THINKING

Complete the multiplication sentence and the division sentence for each picture.

8.

$2 \times 2 =$ ____

$4 \div 2 =$ ____

9.

$3 \times 3 =$ ____

$9 \div 3 =$ ____

10.

$4 \times 4 =$ ____

$16 \div 4 =$ ____

Name _____ Date _____

Connecting Multiplication and Division

Use pictures to solve.

1.

$3 \times 7 =$ _____

$21 \div 7 =$ _____

2.

$5 \times 4 =$ _____

$20 \div 4 =$ _____

Write the fact family for each set of numbers.

3. 4, 6, 24

_____ _____

_____ _____

4. 2, 5, 10

_____ _____

_____ _____

5. 3, 9, 27

_____ _____

_____ _____

MIXED APPLICATIONS

6. There are 18 students in Rosa's class. They are working in groups of 3. Draw a picture on a separate piece of paper to show how many groups there are.

7. Some crayons are divided equally among 3 students. Each student gets 8 crayons. How many crayons are there?

_____

SCIENCE CONNECTION

Each cow's daily feed includes about 4 pounds of food. Tell how many cows could be fed with the following amounts of food.

8. 8 pounds feeds _____ cows.

9. 12 pounds feeds _____ cows.

10. 24 pounds feeds _____ cows.

11. 20 pounds feeds _____ cows.

Inverse Operations: Multiplication and Division

Write a multiplication number sentence and a
division number sentence for each picture.

1.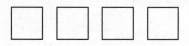

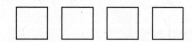

_____ × _____ = _____

_____ ÷ _____ = _____

2.

_____ × _____ = _____

_____ ÷ _____ = _____

Complete. Write a number sentence to show the inverse operation.

3. 36 ÷ 4 = _____   **4.** 5 × _____ = 35   **5.** _____ × 9 = 72

_____   _____   _____

MIXED APPLICATIONS

Circle the correct number sentence. Then solve.

6. Mrs. Panko has 8 tulip bulbs. She plants 2 tulip bulbs
in each flowerpot. How many pots does she use?

8 × 2 = ☐   8 ÷ 2 = ☐

_____

NUMBER SENSE

Complete. Use doubles to help you multiply.

7. 4 fours = 16   **8.** 4 nines = 36   **9.** 3 sixes = 18

So, 8 fours = _____   So, 8 nines = _____   So, 6 sixes = _____

Dividing by 2

Find the quotient.

1.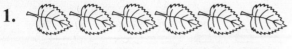

   12 ÷ 2 = _____

2.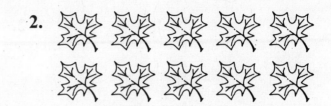

   10 ÷ 2 = _____

Find the missing factor.

3. 2 × _____ = 6   4. _____ × 2 = 12   5. 9 × _____ = 18

Find the quotient.

6. 8 ÷ 2 = _____   7. 4 ÷ 2 = _____   8. 16 ÷ 2 = _____

9. 18 ÷ 2 = _____   10. 2 ÷ 2 = _____   11. 14 ÷ 2 = _____

MIXED APPLICATIONS

12. Kasem earned $3 an hour for raking leaves. It took him 2 hours to do the job. How much money did he earn?

_____

13. The dividend is 12. The divisor is 2. What is the quotient?

_____

MIXED REVIEW

Find the product.

14.	15.	16.	17.	18.	19.
8	9	4	5	7	4
× 3	× 7	× 8	× 9	× 8	× 6

Write the time that is shown.

20.

_____

21.

_____

Name _____   Date _____

Dividing by 3

Write a division sentence for each.

1.

2.

_____   _____

Find the quotient.

3. $12 \div 3 =$ _____   **4.** $18 \div 3 =$ _____   **5.** $21 \div 3 =$ _____   **6.** $8 \div 2 =$ _____

7. $18 \div 2 =$ _____   **8.** $24 \div 3 =$ _____   **9.** $9 \div 3 =$ _____   **10.** $6 \div 3 =$ _____

Write × or ÷ for $\bigcirc$.

11. $15 \bigcirc 3 = 5$ **12.** $4 \bigcirc 2 = 8$ **13.** $9 \bigcirc 3 = 3$ **14.** $3 \bigcirc 7 = 21$

MIXED APPLICATIONS

15. The checkers tournament began at 11:30. It ended 2 hours and 30 minutes later. At what time was it over?

16. At the party after the tournament, Tom spent 65 cents for lemonade, 125 cents for a hot dog, and 95 cents for an apple. How much did Tom spend?

_____   _____

VISUAL THINKING

17. Connect the dots with 6 lines to make 2 squares.

18. Draw 1 more line to make 4 triangles.

64

Dividing by 4

Find the quotient.

1. $24 \div 4 =$ _____   **2.** $15 \div 3 =$ _____   **3.** $12 \div 2 =$ _____   **4.** $16 \div 4 =$ _____

5. $28 \div 4 =$ _____   **6.** $12 \div 4 =$ _____   **7.** $20 \div 4 =$ _____   **8.** $27 \div 3 =$ _____

9. $24 \div 3 =$ _____   **10.** $12 \div 3 =$ _____   **11.** $32 \div 4 =$ _____   **12.** $36 \div 4 =$ _____

13. $4\overline{)12}$ **14.** $4\overline{)8}$ **15.** $3\overline{)9}$ **16.** $2\overline{)16}$ **17.** $4\overline{)24}$ **18.** $3\overline{)15}$

19. $3\overline{)21}$ **20.** $4\overline{)20}$ **21.** $4\overline{)28}$ **22.** $2\overline{)18}$ **23.** $4\overline{)32}$ **24.** $4\overline{)36}$

MIXED APPLICATIONS

25. The third-grade class used rhythm instruments in their show. Twenty-four students shared 6 instruments. How many students shared each instrument?

_____

26. The class sang 8 songs. Each song lasted about 2 minutes. How many minutes did all of the songs take?

_____

NUMBER SENSE

Study the tables. Then write *more* or *fewer* to complete each sentence.

Number of Toys for Each Child			
Toys	3 Children	4 Children	6 Children
24	8	6	4

Number of Acorns for Each Squirrel			
Squirrels	16 Acorns	12 Acorns	8 Acorns
4	4	3	2

27. If the number of toys stays the same, then the more children there are, the _____ toys each child gets.

28. If the number of squirrels stays the same, then the _____ acorns there are, the fewer acorns each squirrel gets.

Dividing by 5

Find the quotient.

1. $5 \overline{)15}$ 2. $4 \overline{)16}$ 3. $5 \overline{)10}$ 4. $2 \overline{)12}$ 5. $5 \overline{)25}$ 6. $4 \overline{)12}$

7. $5 \overline{)20}$ 8. $2 \overline{)10}$ 9. $5 \overline{)30}$ 10. $3 \overline{)18}$ 11. $4 \overline{)28}$ 12. $5 \overline{)45}$

13. $5 \overline{)35}$ 14. $4 \overline{)24}$ 15. $3 \overline{)21}$ 16. $5 \overline{)40}$ 17. $3 \overline{)15}$ 18. $4 \overline{)20}$

19. $25 \div 5 =$ _____   20. $40 \div 5 =$ _____   21. $24 \div 4 =$ _____   22. $18 \div 3 =$ _____

23. $45 \div 5 =$ _____   24. $5 \div 5 =$ _____   25. $16 \div 4 =$ _____   26. $8 \div 2 =$ _____

MIXED APPLICATIONS

27. Sarina made 8 bracelets out of yarn. She used 5 strands of yarn for each bracelet. How many strands of yarn did Sarina use?

_____

28. A skein of yarn is 15 feet long. Sarina needs 3 feet to make a necklace. How many necklaces can Sarina make from one skein?

_____

EVERYDAY MATH CONNECTION

Liza works at an arcade. She trades quarters for nickels so that customers can play the arcade games.

29. Quint has 10 nickels. How many quarters will Liza give Quint?

_____

30. Cai has 25 nickels. How many quarters will Liza give Cai?

_____

31. Liza gives Pat 3 quarters. How many nickels did Pat give to Liza?

_____

32. Wes gives Liza some nickels. She gives Wes 8 quarters. How many nickels did Wes give Liza?

_____

66

Dividing Using 1 and 0

Find the quotient.

1. $2 \div 2 =$ _____   **2.** $0 \div 2 =$ _____   **3.** $7 \div 1 =$ _____   **4.** $20 \div 4 =$ _____

5. $8 \div 1 =$ _____   **6.** $0 \div 5 =$ _____   **7.** $9 \div 9 =$ _____   **8.** $0 \div 4 =$ _____

9. $0 \div 6 =$ _____   **10.** $12 \div 3 =$ _____   **11.** $5 \div 1 =$ _____   **12.** $3 \div 3 =$ _____

13. $6 \div 1 =$ _____   **14.** $8 \div 8 =$ _____   **15.** $27 \div 3 =$ _____   **16.** $7 \div 7 =$ _____

MIXED APPLICATIONS

Write a number sentence and solve.

17. Luis spent 1 hour molding a clay bowl. Then it took him 25 minutes to glaze the bowl. How much longer did Luis spend molding the bowl?

_____

18. There were 8 different glaze colors to choose from. The art teacher had 4 jars of each color. How many jars did the art teacher have?

_____

19. The art teacher placed 87 clay bowls and 18 clay vases in the kiln. How many pieces were in the kiln?

_____

20. Clay is shipped in 36-pound blocks. Each block is divided equally into 9 smaller blocks. How many pounds does each smaller block weigh?

_____

NUMBER SENSE

Complete.

21. $7 \times 4 = 28$, so $28 \div$ _____ $= 7$.   **22.** $9 \times 3 = 27$, so $27 \div$ _____ $= 9$.

23. $8 \times 5 = 40$, so $40 \div$ _____ $= 8$.   **24.** $6 \times 4 = 24$, so $24 \div$ _____ $= 6$.

25. $36 \div 4 = 9$, so $9 \times$ _____ $= 36$.   **26.** $21 \div 3 = 7$, so $7 \times$ _____ $= 21$.

Name _____ Date _____

Division with a Multiplication Table

Use the multiplication table.
Find the missing factor.

×	2	3	4	5	6
2	4	6	8	10	12
3	6	9	12	15	18
4	8	12	16	20	24
5	10	15	20	25	30
6	12	18	24	30	36

1. $5 \times$ _____ $= 20$ **2.** _____ $\times 6 = 24$

3. $2 \times$ _____ $= 10$ **4.** _____ $\times 3 = 9$

Use the table to find the quotient.

5. $16 \div 4 =$ _____   **6.** $30 \div 5 =$ _____   **7.** $8 \div 2 =$ _____   **8.** $36 \div 6 =$ _____

9. $25 \div 5 =$ _____   **10.** $12 \div 4 =$ _____   **11.** $18 \div 6 =$ _____   **12.** $24 \div 6 =$ _____

13. $5\overline{)20}$ **14.** $2\overline{)6}$ **15.** $3\overline{)18}$ **16.** $4\overline{)24}$ **17.** $5\overline{)15}$ **18.** $6\overline{)30}$ **19.** $3\overline{)12}$

MIXED APPLICATIONS

20. A train carries food to several grocery stores. There are 885 cartons of canned goods, 802 cartons of eggs, and 840 cartons of vegetables. Order the cartons from least to greatest.

_____

21. The clerks at Ed's Grocery Store stack the vegetable cartons in the back of the store. They stack 4 rows of cartons. Each row is stacked 8 cartons high. How many vegetable cartons are there?

_____

MIXED REVIEW

Write the time by using numbers and A.M. or P.M.

22. Jason's school starts at twenty minutes after eight. _____

23. Shondra has dinner with her family at six thirty. _____

Write a multiplication and a division fact family for the set of numbers.

24. 4, 3, 12 _____

68

Dividing by 6

Find the quotient.

1. $18 \div 6 =$ _____   2. $54 \div 6 =$ _____   3. $6 \div 6 =$ _____   4. $12 \div 6 =$ _____

5. $20 \div 5 =$ _____   6. $36 \div 6 =$ _____   7. $45 \div 5 =$ _____   8. $42 \div 6 =$ _____

9. $48 \div 6 =$ _____   10. $0 \div 6 =$ _____   11. $30 \div 6 =$ _____   12. $28 \div 4 =$ _____

13. $6\overline{)24}$ 14. $6\overline{)6}$ 15. $6\overline{)18}$ 16. $6\overline{)30}$ 17. $6\overline{)54}$ 18. $6\overline{)0}$

19. $6\overline{)12}$ 20. $5\overline{)40}$ 21. $2\overline{)18}$ 22. $6\overline{)48}$ 23. $4\overline{)24}$ 24. $6\overline{)36}$

25. $5\overline{)30}$ 26. $4\overline{)28}$ 27. $3\overline{)24}$ 28. $2\overline{)16}$ 29. $3\overline{)21}$ 30. $5\overline{)35}$

MIXED APPLICATIONS

31. The quotient is 3 more than the divisor. The dividend is 18. What are the quotient and the divisor?

32. Patti's Pet Store has 24 kittens. They are kept in 6 cages. How many kittens are in each cage?

_____   _____

LOGICAL REASONING

Marnie works in the office of a garden supply store.
She needs to buy 6 pencils for use in the office. She has two choices.

a. pencils that are sold 6 to a box and cost 36¢ a box
b. pencils that are sold separately and cost 8¢ each

33. To spend the least amount of money, should she choose **a** or **b**?
How much money will she save by buying the less expensive pencils?

_____

Unit 7
Core Skills Math, Grade 3

Dividing by 7

Find the quotient.

1. $14 \div 7 =$ _____   **2.** $28 \div 7 =$ _____   **3.** $7 \div 7 =$ _____   **4.** $49 \div 7 =$ _____

5. $42 \div 7 =$ _____   **6.** $21 \div 7 =$ _____   **7.** $63 \div 7 =$ _____   **8.** $56 \div 7 =$ _____

9. $7\overline{)35}$ **10.** $7\overline{)14}$ **11.** $6\overline{)42}$ **12.** $7\overline{)28}$ **13.** $3\overline{)27}$ **14.** $7\overline{)56}$

15. $7\overline{)21}$ **16.** $6\overline{)36}$ **17.** $4\overline{)0}$ **18.** $6\overline{)24}$ **19.** $7\overline{)63}$ **20.** $7\overline{)7}$

Write × or ÷ for ◯ .

21. $7 \bigcirc 9 = 63$ **22.** $42 \bigcirc 7 = 6$ **23.** $36 \bigcirc 6 = 6$ **24.** $8 \bigcirc 2 = 4$

MIXED APPLICATIONS

25. Julio works at a plant nursery. He waters 734 flower plants, 217 bushes, and 48 trees. How many plants does Julio water in all?

26. Mr. Chu buys 9 mum plants. After careful rooting and replanting of these mums, Mr. Chu has 63 mums two years later. If an equal number came from each of the original mums, how many mums did he grow from each original plant?

SCIENCE CONNECTION

A plant gets water through its roots. Then the water moves up the stem to the leaves. In an experiment, a celery stalk was placed in red-colored water. Every hour, the red water traveled another 3 cm up the stalk.

27. How many hours did it take for the red water to travel 12 cm up the celery stalk?

28. If the stalk is 21 cm long, how many hours will it take for the water to travel from one end of the stalk to the other?

Dividing by 8

Find the missing factor.

1. $4 \times$ ____ $= 32$ 2. $5 \times$ ____ $= 0$ 3. ____ $\times 9 = 63$ 4. $8 \times$ ____ $= 48$

Find the quotient.

5. $7 \times 8 = 56$, so $56 \div 8 =$ ____.   6. $3 \times 8 = 24$, so $24 \div 8 =$ ____.

7. $5 \times 8 = 40$, so $40 \div 8 =$ ____.   8. $9 \times 8 = 72$, so $72 \div 8 =$ ____.

9. $2 \times 8 = 16$, so $16 \div 8 =$ ____.   10. $0 \times 8 = 0$, so $0 \div 8 =$ ____.

11. $8\overline{)24}$ 12. $6\overline{)24}$ 13. $5\overline{)40}$ 14. $7\overline{)42}$ 15. $8\overline{)56}$ 16. $5\overline{)5}$

17. $4\overline{)36}$ 18. $8\overline{)48}$ 19. $4\overline{)32}$ 20. $5\overline{)45}$ 21. $8\overline{)72}$ 22. $8\overline{)64}$

MIXED APPLICATIONS

23. Ms. West's third grade is having a math-a-thon. Each student is asked to complete a 72-problem booklet in 8 days. Millie will do the same number of problems each day. How many problems will she do each day?

_____

24. Millie sees that 3 pages in the math booklet each have 9 addition problems and 4 pages each have 7 subtraction problems. Are there more addition or more subtraction problems in the booklet?

_____

MIXED REVIEW

Find the sum or difference.

25. 345
     $+ 482$

26. 901
        23
      $+ \ 9$

27. 29
        75
      $+ 43$

28. 809
     $- 397$

29. 400
     $- 156$

Dividing by 9

Find the quotient.

1. 54 ÷ 9 = ____   2. 36 ÷ 9 = ____   3. 81 ÷ 9 = ____   4. 27 ÷ 3 = ____

5. 18 ÷ 9 = ____   6. 72 ÷ 8 = ____   7. 48 ÷ 6 = ____   8. 21 ÷ 7 = ____

9. $9\overline{)36}$ 10. $7\overline{)42}$ 11. $9\overline{)81}$ 12. $7\overline{)63}$ 13. $9\overline{)9}$ 14. $7\overline{)56}$

15. $8\overline{)48}$ 16. $9\overline{)45}$ 17. $9\overline{)0}$ 18. $9\overline{)63}$ 19. $6\overline{)54}$ 20. $9\overline{)27}$

MIXED APPLICATIONS

21. The Springdale Sports Club has 63 students signed up for baseball teams. There are 7 equal-size teams formed. How many students are on each team?

_____

22. One baseball team collects $5 from each of its 9 players to buy the coach a gift. How much money is collected?

_____

23. One factor is 2 less than the other. The product is 48. What are the factors?

_____

24. In one game, Kristi scores 4 more runs than Jon. Jon scores 1 run fewer than Carlos. Carlos scores 3 runs. How many runs do Jon and Kristi each score?

_____

WRITER'S CORNER

25. Write a problem that you can solve by dividing by 9.

_____

_____

_____

The Division Facts

Find the quotient.

1. $3 \times 9 = 27$, so $27 \div 9 =$ _____.   **2.** $6 \times 4 = 24$, so $24 \div 4 =$ _____.

3. $2 \times 8 = 16$, so $8\overline{)16} =$ _____.   **4.** $5 \times 9 = 45$, so $9\overline{)45} =$ _____.

5. $6\overline{)36}$ **6.** $4\overline{)24}$ **7.** $1\overline{)9}$ **8.** $9\overline{)81}$ **9.** $7\overline{)49}$ **10.** $5\overline{)30}$

11. $3\overline{)3}$ **12.** $2\overline{)18}$ **13.** $8\overline{)32}$ **14.** $8\overline{)56}$ **15.** $7\overline{)14}$ **16.** $6\overline{)6}$

17. $9\overline{)54}$ **18.** $1\overline{)7}$ **19.** $4\overline{)0}$ **20.** $2\overline{)4}$ **21.** $3\overline{)24}$ **22.** $5\overline{)10}$

23. $6\overline{)48}$ **24.** $5\overline{)35}$ **25.** $2\overline{)12}$ **26.** $4\overline{)36}$ **27.** $8\overline{)16}$ **28.** $3\overline{)21}$

29. $8\overline{)40}$ **30.** $9\overline{)45}$ **31.** $1\overline{)5}$ **32.** $7\overline{)0}$ **33.** $5\overline{)15}$ **34.** $6\overline{)18}$

MIXED APPLICATIONS

35. There are 44 students and 12 adults going on a school field trip. They will take 8-person vans for the trip. How many vans will they need?

36. Parking for each van costs $6. How much does parking cost for the field trip?

Make a Model

Work with a group. Use counters to model each problem. Give an equal number to each person in the group. Write how many counters each person gets.

1. There are 48 toy dinosaurs. There are 6 people in the group. How many dinosaurs does each person get?

   _____

2. There are 28 blocks. There are 7 people in the group. How many blocks does each person get?

   _____

3. There are 12 toy cars. There are 6 people in the group. How many cars does each person get?

   _____

4. There are 45 crayons. There are 5 people in the group. How many crayons does each person get?

   _____

LOGICAL REASONING

5. Marcie collects 5 shells every day for 3 days. Adam collects 4 shells every day for 4 days. Who collects more shells?

   _____

6. Susan draws a picture that has 3 rows of 7 stars. Tito draws a picture that has 4 rows of 5 stars. Who draws more stars?

   _____

7. Zack has a box of 16 raisins. He wants to make equal groups of raisins. Circle the numbers that he can have in each equal group.

   2   4   5   6   8   9

8. Roberto has 36 whistles to give to the guests at his party. If 8 guests are at the party, can he give each guest an equal number and give away all of the whistles? Write *yes* or *no*.

   _____

74

Problem Solving

MODEL DIVISION

Use models to solve each problem.

1. Six customers at a toy store bought 18 jump ropes. Each customer bought the same number of jump ropes. How many jump ropes did each customer buy?

   _____

2. Hiro has 36 pictures of his summer trip. He wants to put them in an album. Each page of the album holds 4 pictures. How many pages will Hiro need for his pictures?

   _____

3. Katia has 42 crayons in a box. She buys a storage bin that has 6 sections. She puts the same number of crayons in each section. How many crayons does Katia put in each section of the storage bin?

   _____

4. Ms. Taylor's students give cards to each of the 3 class parent helpers. There are 24 cards. How many cards will each helper get if the students give an equal number of cards to each helper?

   _____

5. Jamie divides 20 baseball stickers equally among 5 of his friends. How many stickers does each friend get?

   _____

Find Unknown Factors

Find the unknown factor.

1. $n \times 3 = 12$

Think: How many groups of 3 equal 12?

$n =$ _____

2. $s \times 8 = 64$

$s =$ _____

3. $21 = 7 \times n$

$n =$ _____

4. $y \times 2 = 18$

$y =$ _____

5. $5 \times p = 10$

$p =$ _____

6. $56 = 8 \times t$

$t =$ _____

7. $m \times 4 = 28$

$m =$ _____

8. $\bigstar \times 1 = 9$

$\bigstar =$ _____

9. $18 = 6 \times r$

$r =$ _____

10. $u \times 5 = 30$

$u =$ _____

11. $4 \times \blacksquare = 24$

$\blacksquare =$ _____

12. $w \times 7 = 35$

$w =$ _____

13. $b \times 6 = 54$

$b =$ _____

14. $5 \times \blacktriangle = 40$

$\blacktriangle =$ _____

15. $30 = d \times 3$

$d =$ _____

16. $7 \times k = 42$

$k =$ _____

PROBLEM SOLVING

17. Carmen spent \$42 for 6 hats. How much did each hat cost?

_____

18. Mark has a baking tray with 24 muffins. The muffins are arranged in 4 equal rows. How many muffins are in each row?

_____

76

Divide by 8

Find the unknown factor and quotient.

1. $8 \times$ ____ $= 32$ $32 \div 8 =$ ____   **2.** $3 \times$ ____ $= 27$ $27 \div 3 =$ ____

3. $8 \times$ ____ $= 8$ $8 \div 8 =$ ____   **4.** $8 \times$ ____ $= 72$ $72 \div 8 =$ ____

Find the quotient.

5. ____ $= 24 \div 8$ **6.** $40 \div 8 =$ ____   **7.** ____ $= 56 \div 8$ **8.** $14 \div 2 =$ ____

9. $8\overline{)64}$ **10.** $7\overline{)28}$ **11.** $8\overline{)16}$ **12.** $8\overline{)48}$

Find the unknown number.

13. $16 \div p = 8$ **14.** $25 \div \blacksquare = 5$ **15.** $24 \div a = 3$ **16.** $k \div 10 = 8$

$p =$ ____ $\blacksquare =$ ____ $a =$ ____ $k =$ ____

PROBLEM SOLVING

17. Sixty-four students are going on a field trip. There is 1 adult for every 8 students. How many adults are there?

_____

18. Mr. Chen spends $32 for tickets to a play. If the tickets cost $8 each, how many tickets does Mr. Chen buy?

_____

77

Exploring Divisibility

Circle the numbers that fit the divisibility rule.

1. Every even number is divisible by 2. Which of these numbers can be divided by 2?

    4   28   31   45   52

2. A number can be divided by 3 if the digits add up to a multiple of 3, such as 3, 6, or 9. Which of these numbers can be divided by 3?

    12   18   23   24   28

3. A number is divisible by 5 if it ends with 5 or 0. Which of these numbers can be divided by 5?

    12   20   25   35   47

4. A number is divisible by 10 if it ends with 0. Which of these numbers can be divided by 10?

    15   30   36   50   65

Is the first number divisible by the second number? Write *yes* or *no*.

5. 15, 5 _____   **6.** 27, 3 _____   **7.** 45, 2 _____   **8.** 70, 10 _____

MIXED APPLICATIONS

9. There are 21 students divided equally among 7 math tutors. How many students are with each tutor?

_____

10. If 5 friends share 30 marbles equally, how many marbles does each person get?

_____

LOGICAL REASONING

Write *yes* or *no*.

11. If a number is divisible by 2, is it ever divisible by an odd number?

_____

12. If a number is divisible by 10, is it ever divisible by 3?

_____

13. If a number is divisible by 10, is it always divisible by 5?

_____

14. If a number is divisible by 5, is it always divisible by 10?

_____

78

Exploring Division Patterns

Use patterns to complete each place-value chart.

1.

Place-Value Chart

	Hundreds	Tens	Ones
8 ÷ 4	X	X	2
80 ÷ 4	X		X
800 ÷ 4		X	X

2.

Place-Value Chart

	Hundreds	Tens	Ones
20 ÷ 5			
200 ÷ 5			
2,000 ÷ 5			

Use mental math to find the quotient.

3. $8 \div 4 =$ _____

4. $80 \div 4 =$ _____

5. $800 \div 4 =$ _____

6. $20 \div 5 =$ _____

7. $200 \div 5 =$ _____

8. $2,000 \div 5 =$ _____

9. $24 \div 4 =$ _____

10. $240 \div 4 =$ _____

11. $2,400 \div 4 =$ _____

12. $35 \div 5 =$ _____

13. $350 \div 5 =$ _____

14. $3,500 \div 5 =$ _____

EVERYDAY MATH CONNECTION

Use mental math to solve. Use a calculator to check.

15. The library has 1,600 books to sell. An equal number of books are placed into 8 bookcases. How many books are in each bookcase?

_____

16. The same number of books is placed on each shelf. If each bookcase has 4 shelves, how many books are on each shelf?

_____

Exploring Plane Figures

Name the figure that each object looks like.

1.

_____

2.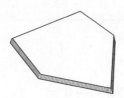

_____

3.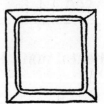

_____

4.

_____

5.

_____

6.

_____

Draw a line from the description to the figure. Each figure is used once.

7. 4 sides and 4 corners
   All sides are the same length.

8. 4 sides and 4 corners
   All sides are not the same length.

9. 3 sides and 3 corners

10. 0 sides and 0 corners

11. 5 sides and 5 corners

rectangle

circle

pentagon

square

triangle

EVERYDAY MATH CONNECTION

Name two things in the kitchen of your home that are shaped like each figure listed.

12. Square   _____   _____

13. Rectangle   _____   _____

14. Circle   _____   _____

Classify Quadrilaterals

Circle all the words that describe the quadrilateral.

1.

square

rectangle

rhombus

trapezoid

2.

square

rectangle

rhombus

trapezoid

3.

square

rectangle

rhombus

trapezoid

Use the quadrilaterals below for 4–6.

 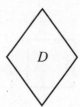

A B C D E

4. Which quadrilaterals appear to have no right angles?

_____

5. Which quadrilaterals appear to have 4 right angles?

_____

6. Which quadrilaterals appear to have 4 sides of equal length?

_____

PROBLEM SOLVING

7. A picture on the wall in Jeremy's classroom has 4 right angles, 4 sides of equal length, and 2 pairs of opposite sides that are parallel. Which quadrilateral(s) best describe the picture?

_____

8. Sofia has a plate that has 4 sides of equal length, 2 pairs of opposite sides that are parallel, and no right angles. What quadrilateral best describes the plate?

_____

Draw Quadrilaterals

Draw a quadrilateral that is described. Name the quadrilateral you drew.

1. 4 sides of equal length

_____

2. 1 pair of opposite sides that are parallel

_____

Draw a quadrilateral that does not belong. Then explain why.

3.

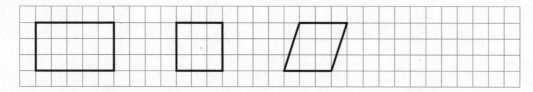

_____

_____

_____

PROBLEM SOLVING

4. Layla drew a quadrilateral with 4 right angles and 2 pairs of opposite sides that are parallel. Name the quadrilateral she could have drawn.

_____

5. Victor drew a quadrilateral with no right angles and 4 sides of equal length. What quadrilateral could Victor have drawn?

_____

Describe Triangles

Use triangles *A*, *B*, and *C* for Exercises 1–3. Complete the sentences.

1. Triangle _____ has 3 angles less than a right angle and

   appears to have _____ sides of equal length.

2. Triangle _____ has 1 right angle and appears to have

   _____ sides of equal length.

3. Triangle _____ has 1 angle greater than a right angle and

   appears to have _____ sides of equal length.

4. Kyle, Kathy, and Kelly each drew a
   triangle. Who drew the triangle that has
   1 angle greater than a right angle and
   appears to have no sides of equal length?

   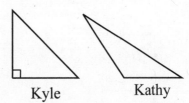

   _____

PROBLEM SOLVING

5. Matthew drew the back of his tent.
   How many sides appear to be of
   equal length?

   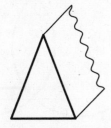

   _____

6. Sierra made the triangular picture
   frame shown. How many angles are
   greater than a right angle?

   _____

Problem Solving

CLASSIFY PLANE SHAPES

Solve each problem.

1. Steve drew the shapes below. Write the letter of each shape where it belongs in the Venn diagram.

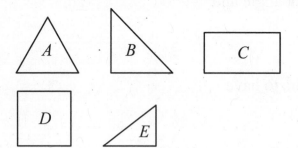

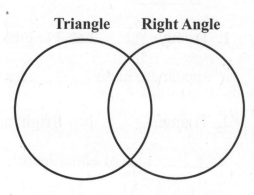

Triangle   **Right Angle**

2. Janice drew the shapes below. Write the letter of each shape where it belongs in the Venn diagram.

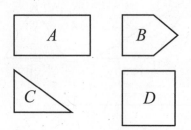

Right Angle   **All Sides of Equal Length**

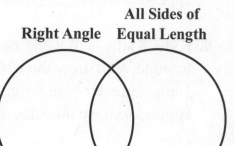

3. Beth drew the shapes below. Write the letter of each shape where it belongs in the Venn diagram.

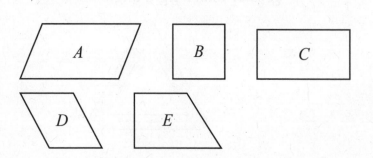

Parallel Sides   **Perpendicular Sides**

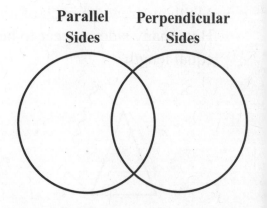

Introduction to Perimeter

Use your ruler to measure each side to the nearest centimeter. Add the length of each side to measure the perimeter.

1.

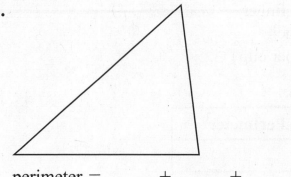

perimeter = _____ + _____ + _____ = _____ centimeters

2.

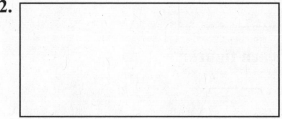

perimeter = _____ + _____ + _____ + _____ = _____ cm

3.

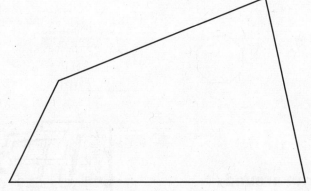

perimeter = _____ + _____ + _____ + _____ = _____ cm

LOGICAL REASONING

4. Paco has a square stamp that is 6 centimeters wide.

The perimeter of the stamp is _____ centimeters.

Exploring Perimeter

Choose a book from your desk, classroom, or home. Find its perimeter three times. Each time use a different unit of measure. Use the units of measure in the list below.

       a. width of your finger
       b. width of a pencil
       c. width of a paper clip

Complete the table.

	Unit of Measure	Guess	Perimeter
1.	Finger width		
2.	Pencil width		
3.	Clip width		

Use the width of a crayon. Find the perimeter of each figure.

4. _____ units

5. 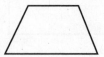 _____ units

6. _____ units

7. _____ units

CAREER CONNECTION

James is a carpenter. He is putting wood trim around the window in a hallway. He needs to know the perimeter of the window so that he can buy the correct amount of wood.

8. Write a sentence describing how James could use a ruler to find the perimeter.

_____

_____

Name _____ Date _____

Measuring Perimeter

Use an inch ruler and a string to find the perimeter of each.

1. your chair seat _____

2. a library book _____

3. a calculator _____

4. a folder _____

Write a number sentence to find the perimeter of each figure. Solve.

5.

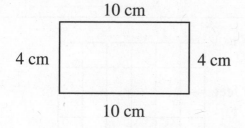

10 cm

4 cm   4 cm

10 cm

_____

_____

6.

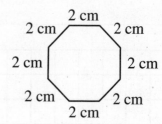

2 cm
2 cm   2 cm
2 cm   2 cm
2 cm   2 cm
2 cm

_____

_____

Solve. You may use a calculator.

7. A rectangle is 6 in. long and 12 in. wide. Find the perimeter.

_____

8. A square measures 13 cm on each side. Find the perimeter.

_____

MIXED REVIEW

Find the product.

9.	10.	11.	12.	13.	14.
90	31	12	25	87	157
×2	×3	×2	×4	×1	×0

15. Dave's train ride started at 11:30 A.M. and ended at 12:30 P.M. How much time did the train ride take?

_____

Core Skills Math, Grade 3

Finding Perimeter

Find the perimeter of each figure.

1.

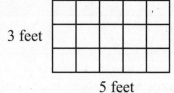

3 feet

5 feet

2.

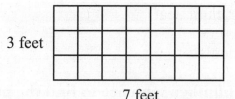

3 feet

7 feet

3.

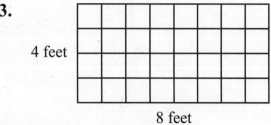

4 feet

8 feet

4.

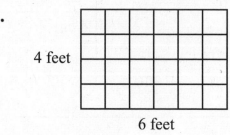

4 feet

6 feet

5.

10 cm

4 cm   4 cm

10 cm

6.

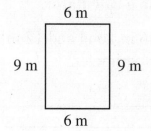

6 m

9 m   9 m

6 m

ART CONNECTION

7. One of the most famous paintings in the world
is the Mona Lisa, by Leonardo da Vinci. It is about
31 inches tall and about 21 inches wide. What is
the perimeter of the painting?

Name _____ Date _____

Using Perimeter

Find the perimeter of each picture.

1.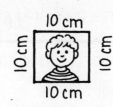

10 cm
10 cm
10 cm
10 cm

_____

2.

90 feet

80 feet

_____

3.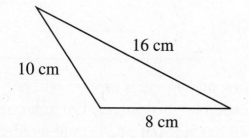

16 cm
10 cm
8 cm

_____

4.

7 cm
7 cm   7 cm
7 cm

_____

5.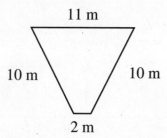

11 m
10 m   10 m
2 m

_____

6.

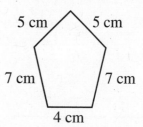

5 cm   5 cm
7 cm   7 cm
4 cm

_____

MIXED APPLICATIONS

7. Steve put together a jigsaw puzzle that is 14 inches wide and 16 inches tall. What is the perimeter of the puzzle?

_____

8. Adelita has 32 inches of wood trim to make a square picture frame. If she uses all of the wood, how long is each side of the frame?

_____

89

Perimeter of a Triangle

Draw a picture and write the lengths of each side. Solve.

1. Tammy makes a picture frame that is a triangle. Each side is 6 inches long. What is the perimeter?

2. Marco has a triangular garden with two sides that are 8 feet long and one side that is 11 feet long. What is the perimeter?

_____   _____

3. Roger needs trim for a bandana that is a triangle. The bandana measures 20 inches on the longest side and 15 inches on the other sides. How much trim does he need?

4. How many meters of wire will be needed to go around a triangular park that has sides of 50, 45, and 69 meters?

_____   _____

5. What is the perimeter of a triangular play area that has sides that are 8 yards, 6 yards, and 10 yards long?

6. Mr. Wong puts bricks around his triangular garden. Each brick is 1 foot long. The sides of the garden are 30, 20, and 40 feet. How many bricks does he need?

_____   _____

Perimeter of a Rectangle

Draw a picture of each rectangle and write the length and width. Solve.

1. Ned wants to fence his garden. It is 12 feet long and 10 feet wide. How much fencing does he need?

2. The park near Ned's house is 55 meters long and 40 meters wide. What is the perimeter of the park?

_____

3. The Madison Farm measures 1,000 yards by 1,000 yards. How many feet of fencing will it take to fence the entire farm?

4. April made a pillow that is 51 centimeters long and 39 centimeters wide. How much trim does she need to go around the pillow?

_____

5. The top of Mr. Montoya's desk is 64 inches long and 30 inches wide. What is the perimeter of the top of the desk?

6. Lin's bedroom window is twice as long as it is wide. It is 30 inches wide. What is the perimeter?

_____

91

Understand Area

Count to find the area of the shape.

1.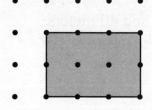

Area = ____ square units

2.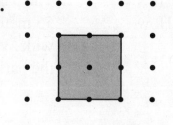

Area = ____ square units

3.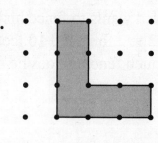

Area = ____ square units

4.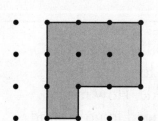

Area = ____ square units

5.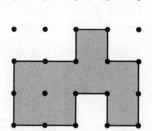

Area = ____ square units

6.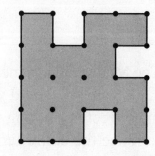

Area = ____ square units

Write *area* or *perimeter* for each situation.

7. carpeting a floor

8. fencing a garden

_____   _____

PROBLEM SOLVING

Use the diagram for 9–10.

9. Roberto is building a platform for his model railroad. What is the area of the platform?

_____

10. Roberto will put a border around the edges of the platform. How much border will he need?

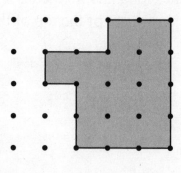

_____

Measure Area

Count to find the area of the shape. Each unit square is 1 square centimeter.

1.

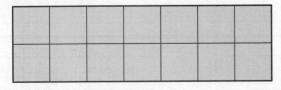

Area = _____ square centimeters

2.

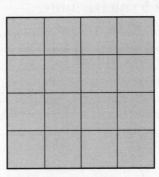

Area = _____ square centimeters

3.

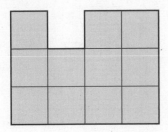

Area = _____ square centimeters

4.

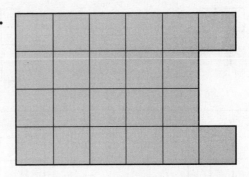

Area = _____ square centimeters

PROBLEM SOLVING

Alan is painting his deck gray. Use the diagram at the right for 5–6. Each unit square is 1 square meter.

Alan's Deck

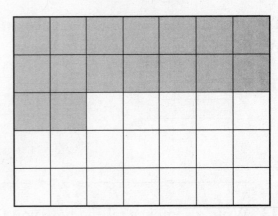

5. What is the area of the deck that Alan has already painted gray?

_____

6. What is the area of the deck that Alan has left to paint?

_____

Exploring Area

Fill in squares with your pencil. Make three shapes, each with an area of 6 square units.

1.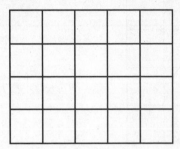

2.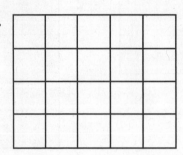

3.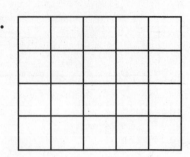

Find the area of each figure. Label your answer in square units.

4.

5.

6.

_____ _____ _____

7.

8.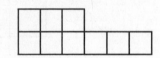

9.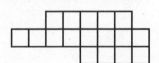

_____ _____ _____

VISUAL THINKING

The area of this figure is 4 square units.
Write the area of each figure below.

10.

11.

12.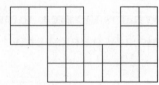

_____ _____ _____

13. Write a sentence telling how you found your answers.

_____

_____

Name _____   Date _____

Use Area Models

Find the area of each shape. Each unit square is 1 square foot.

1.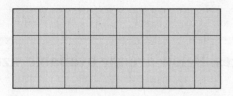

2.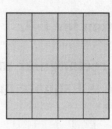

_____

Find the area of each shape. Each unit square is 1 square meter.

3.    4. 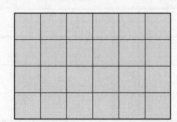   5.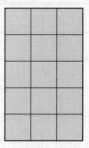

_____   _____   _____

| **PROBLEM SOLVING** |

6. Landon made a rug for the hallway. Each unit square is 1 square foot. What is the area of the rug?

7. Eva makes a border at the top of a picture frame. Each unit square is 1 square inch. What is the area of the border?

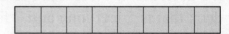

_____   _____

95

Unit 10
Core Skills Math, Grade 3

Problem Solving

AREA OF RECTANGLES

Use the information for 1–3.

An artist makes rectangular murals in different sizes. Below are the available sizes. Each unit square is 1 square meter.

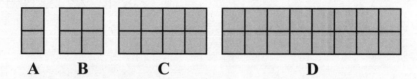

A   B   C   D

1. Complete the table to find the area of each mural.

Mural	Length (in meters)	Width (in meters)	Area (in square meters)
A	2	1	
B	2		
C	2		
D	2		

2. Find and describe a pattern of how the length changes and how the width changes for murals A through D.

_____

_____

3. How do the areas of the murals change when the width changes?

_____

_____

4. Dan built a deck that is 5 feet long and 5 feet wide. He built another deck that is 5 feet long and 7 feet wide. He built a third deck that is 5 feet long and 9 feet wide. How do the areas change?

_____

_____

Name _____ Date _____

Finding Area of Rectangles

Multiply length times width to find the area of each rectangle.

1.
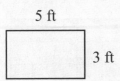
5 ft

3 ft

$5 \times 3 = 15$ square ft

2.
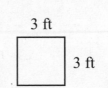
3 ft

3 ft

_____

3.
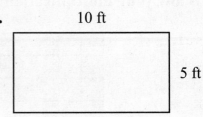
10 ft

5 ft

_____

4.
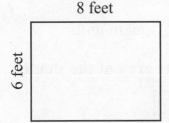
8 feet

6 feet

_____

5.
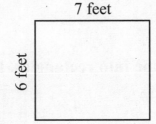
7 feet

6 feet

_____

6.
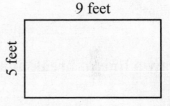
9 feet

5 feet

_____

MIXED APPLICATIONS

7. Mr. Lee's kitchen is 9 feet long and 8 feet wide. What is the area of his kitchen?

_____

8. The rug in Mr. Lee's classroom is 6 feet long and 4 feet wide. What is the area of the rug?

_____

9. Ms. Sand's classroom is 9 meters long and 6 meters wide. What is the area of her classroom?

_____

10. The picture on Ms. Sand's desk is 8 centimeters long and 5 centimeters wide. What is the area of the picture?

_____

LOGICAL REASONING

11. Two posters have equal heights. One poster is a square, and the other is a rectangle twice as long as it is high. Which poster has the greater area?

_____

Area of Combined Rectangles

Use the Distributive Property to find the area.
Show your multiplication and addition equations.

1.

$4 \times 2 = 8; 4 \times 5 = 20$
_____

$8 + 20 = 28$
_____

___28___ square units

2.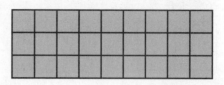

_____

_____

_____ square units

Draw a line to break apart the shape into rectangles. Find the area of the shape.

3.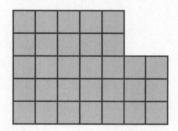

Rectangle 1: _____ × _____ = _____

Rectangle 2: _____ × _____ = _____

_____ + _____ = _____ square units

4.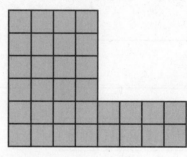

Rectangle 1: _____ × _____ = _____

Rectangle 2: _____ × _____ = _____

_____ + _____ = _____ square units

PROBLEM SOLVING

A diagram of Frank's room is at right.
Each unit square is 1 square foot.

5. Draw a line to divide the shape of
Frank's room into rectangles.

6. What is the total area of Frank's room?

_____ square feet

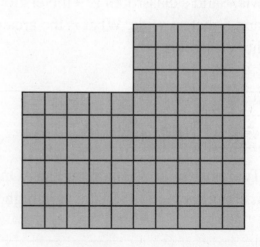

Exploring Relating Perimeter and Area

Solve. Find the perimeter and area of each rectangle.

1.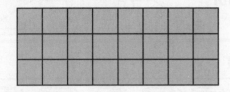

2.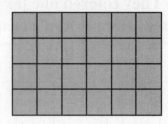

$P =$ ___ + ___ + ___ + ___ = ___ $P =$ ___ + ___ + ___ + ___ = ___

$A =$ ___ × ___ = ___ $A =$ ___ × ___ = ___

Draw two rectangles that have the same perimeter but different areas.

3.

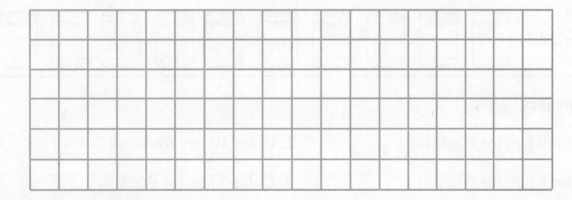

LOGICAL REASONING

Use the picture to solve.

4. Find the perimeter and area of the rectangle.
   Circle the number that is greater.

   $P =$ _____

   $A =$ _____

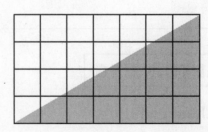

5. Is the perimeter of the triangle or the area
   of the triangle half of the rectangle?

Make a Picture Graph

A group of children collected jars. Then they each
made a graph. They colored one jar on the graph for
each jar collected. Here is Ken's graph.

Jars Collected

Color the jars.

1. Color 9 jars for Week 1.

2. Color 10 jars for Week 2.

3. Color 8 jars for Week 3.

4. Color 5 jars for Week 4.

Find the sum or difference.

5. How many jars did Ken collect in all
for Weeks 2 and 3?

6. How many more jars did Ken collect in
Week 1 than in Week 4?

VISUAL THINKING

Solve without counting.

7. In which week did Ken collect the
fewest jars?

8. In which week did Ken collect the
most jars?

Understand Picture Graphs

Use the Math Test Scores picture graph for 1–7.

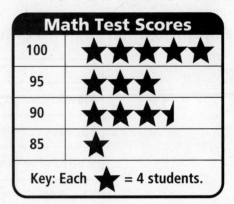

Mrs. Perez made a picture graph of her students' scores on a math test.

1. How many students scored 100? How can you find the answer?

   _____

   _____

   _____

2. What does ★ stand for?

   _____

3. How many students in all scored 100 or 95?

   _____

4. How many more students scored 90 than 85?

   _____

5. How many students in all took the test?

   _____

PROBLEM SOLVING

6. Suppose the students who scored 85 and 90 on the math test take the test again and score 95. How many stars would you have to add to the picture graph next to 95?

   _____

7. If 2 more students took the math test and both scored 80, what would the picture graph look like?

   _____

   _____

101

Use Pictographs

Use the pictograph and the key for Exercises 1–3.

Number of Shirts Sold	
Monday	👕 👕 👕 👕 👕 👕
Tuesday	👕 👕 👕 👕
Wednesday	👕 👕
Thursday	👕 👕 👕 👕
Friday	👕 👕 👕 👕 👕 👕 👕 👕

👕 = 10 shirts

1. On which day were the fewest shirts sold? _____

2. Were more shirts sold Tuesday or Friday? _____

3. How many shirts were sold on Monday? _____

MIXED APPLICATIONS

Use the pictograph and the key for Exercises 4–5.

4. How many more boxes of buttons were used on Monday than on Thursday?

_____

5. The shirt factory pays $1 for each box of buttons. How much did it spend on buttons on Friday?

_____

Boxes of Buttons Used	
Monday	◉ ◉ ◉ ◉ ◉ ◉ ◉
Tuesday	◉ ◉ ◉ ◉
Wednesday	◉ ◉
Thursday	◉ ◉ ◉
Friday	◉ ◉ ◉ ◉ ◉

◉ = 10 boxes of buttons

VISUAL THINKING

If ● stands for 10 boxes of buttons, then ◖ stands for 5 boxes of buttons. Tell the number of boxes of buttons shown.

6. ● ● ● ◖ _____

7. ● ● ● ● ◖ ● ● ◖ _____

More Using Pictographs

Use the pictograph for Exercises 1–4.

Votes for Class President	
Person	**Number of Votes**
Fran	☐☐☐☐☐☐☐☐⧘
Ben	☐☐☐☐☐☐
Crissy	☐☐☐☐☐☐☐☐☐
Anil	☐☐☐☐☐☐
Angelina	☐☐☐☐⧘

☐ = 10 votes

1. Which two students got the same number of votes?

   _____

2. Who got the most votes?

   _____

3. How many votes did Fran get?

   _____

4. What was the total number of votes for Angelina and Crissy?

   _____

MIXED APPLICATIONS

5. If the key in a pictograph has a symbol that stands for 3 students, how many symbols would you need to represent 24 students?

   _____

6. If the key in a pictograph has a symbol that stands for 10 students, how many symbols would you need to represent 25 students?

   _____

LOGICAL REASONING

7. Sanjaya's pictograph shows library books borrowed by adults and children. He uses a square to stand for 2 books. He uses 20 squares in all. If adults took out 4 more books than children, how many books did children take out?

   _____

Reading a Bar Graph

Use the bar graph for Exercises 1–2.

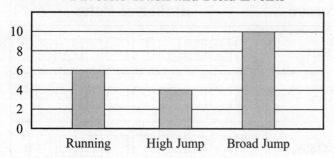

Favorite Track and Field Events

1. Which event is the favorite?

_____

2. How many more students voted for the broad jump than for the high jump?

_____

MIXED APPLICATIONS

Choose a strategy and solve.

> **STRATEGIES**
> • Act it Out • Draw a Picture
> • Write a Number Sentence • Work Backward

3. Della bought a soccer ball that was marked down from $10 to $7. How much money did Della save by buying the ball at the marked-down price?

_____

4. Juanita measures her new tennis racket. The stringed head is 9 inches. The handle is 11 inches. What is the racket's length?

_____

5. A square field measures 6 yards on each side. What is the perimeter of the field?

_____

6. On Saturday, Tad jogged from 1:55 to 2:40. For how long did Tad jog?

_____

VISUAL THINKING

7. Mr. Ming may swim the perimeter of Pool A or Pool B. In which pool will he swim farther? How much farther?

_____

_____

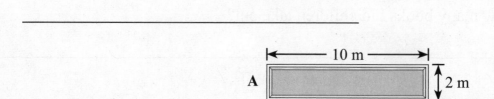

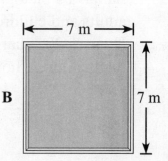

104

Name _____   Date _____

Exploring Bar Graphs

Use the After-Dinner Activities bar graph for 1–6.

The third-grade students at Case Elementary School were asked what they spent the most time doing last week after dinner. The results are shown in the bar graph at the right.

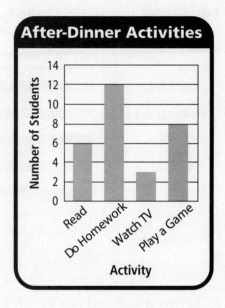

After-Dinner Activities

1. How many students spent the most time watching TV after dinner?

   _____

2. How many students in all answered the survey?

   _____

3. How many students in all played a game or read?

   _____

4. How many fewer students read than did homework?

   _____

5. How many more students read than watched TV?

   _____

PROBLEM SOLVING

6. Suppose 3 students changed their answers to reading instead of doing homework. Where would the bar for reading end?

   _____

Name _____ Date _____

Understanding Bar Graphs

The art teacher asked students which art project they want to work on.
A bar graph shows the results. Use this graph to answer Exercises 1–6.

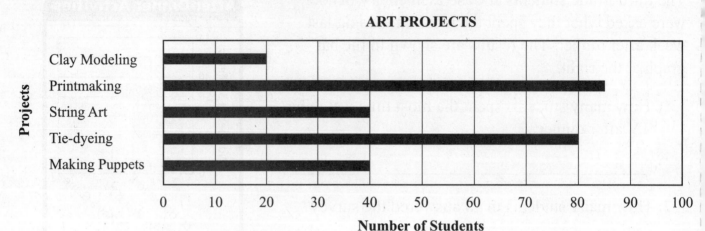

ART PROJECTS

1. Is this a vertical bar graph or a horizontal bar graph? _____

2. What do the numbers below the graph show? _____

3. What does each interval of the scale represent? _____

4. Which project was most popular? _____

5. Which project was least popular? _____

6. How many students chose printmaking or tie-dyeing? _____

MIXED REVIEW

Write the three other facts for each fact family.

7. $8 \times 6 = 48$ 8. $56 \div 7 = 8$ 9. $6 \times 7 = 42$

_____   _____   _____

_____   _____   _____

_____   _____   _____

Using Bar Graphs

Use the bar graph about monthly television sales for Exercises 1–6.

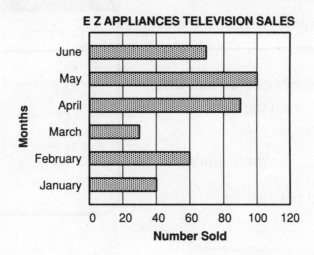

E Z APPLIANCES TELEVISION SALES

1. What scale is shown on the graph?

    _____

2. Were more televisions sold in January or in March?

    _____

3. How many televisions were sold in June?

    _____

4. In what month were more than 70 but fewer than 100 sold?

    _____

5. How many more televisions were sold in May than in March?

    _____

6. How many televisions in all were sold in January and February?

    _____

EVERYDAY MATH CONNECTION

7. Make a bar graph to show the favorite sport of 10 people. Choose a scale, title, and label for your graph. Then color in the bars.

Unit 11
Core Skills Math, Grade 3

Solve Problems Using Bar Graphs

Use the Favorite Hot Lunch bar graph for 1–3.

1. How many more students chose pizza than chose grilled cheese?

   Think: Subtract the number of students who chose grilled cheese, 2, from the number of students who chose pizza, 11.

   $11 - 2 = 9$ _____ more students

2. How many students did not choose chicken patty?

   _____ students

3. How many fewer students chose grilled cheese than chose hot dog?

   _____ fewer students

Use the Ways to Get to School bar graph for 4–7.

4. How many more students walk than ride in a car to get to school?

   _____ more students

5. How many students walk and ride a bike combined?

   _____ students

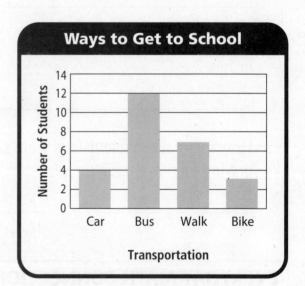

PROBLEM SOLVING

6. Is the number of students who get to school by car and bus greater than or less than the number of students who get to school by walking and biking? Explain.

   _____

   _____

7. If 5 more students respond that they get to school by biking, would more students walk or ride a bike to school? Explain.

   _____

   _____

108

Exploring Making a Bar Graph

Will and his friends earned money during the summer.

1. Use the table to make a bar graph. Remember:

   • Choose a scale.
   • Label the graph.
   • Write a title for the graph.

Lawns Mowed This Summer	
Name	**Number**
Will	6
Taylor	10
Joaquin	8
Barb	4
Steve	3

Use the graph you made to help you answer Exercises 2–3.

2. Who mowed the greatest number of lawns?

   _____

3. How many lawns did Will and his friends mow in all?

   _____

WRITER'S CORNER

4. Take a survey of your friends' favorite summer activities. Make a bar graph on a separate piece of paper to show the information. Explain what the bar graph shows.

   _____

109

Make a Bar Graph

The class took a survey to find out the different ways the students in their grade got to school. They made a table of the data.

Transportation to School	
Type	**Number of Students**
Bus	18
Car	5
Walk	7
Bicycle	10

1. Make a bar graph using the information from the table. Remember to:
   • decide whether you want a vertical or horizontal graph.
   • choose a scale.
   • label the graph.
   • write a title for the graph.

MIXED APPLICATIONS

STRATEGIES
• Find a Pattern • Choose the Operation • Work Backward
• Make a Table • Write a Number Sentence

Choose a strategy and solve.

2. Clara bought 2 books. Each book cost $6. Then she spent $10 for a CD. How much money did Clara start with if she had $4 left?

3. The PTA members are raising money for a bicycle rack that costs $225. They raise $125 the first week. How many weeks will it take to raise what is left if they get $20 each week?

WRITER'S CORNER

4. Survey your friends to find out how they get to school. Make a bar graph on a separate piece of paper to show the results. Explain what your graph shows.

Name _____ Date _____

Use and Make Line Plots

Use the data in the table to make a line plot.

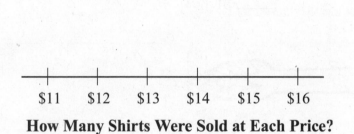

$11 $12 $13 $14 $15 $16
How Many Shirts Were Sold at Each Price?

How Many Shirts Were Sold at Each Price?	
Price	Number Sold
$11	1
$12	4
$13	6
$14	4
$15	0
$16	2

1. How many shirts sold for $12?

_____

2. At which price were the most shirts sold?

_____

3. How many shirts in all were sold?

_____

4. How many shirts were sold for $13 or more?

_____

PROBLEM SOLVING

Use the line plot above for 5–6.

5. Were more shirts sold for less than $13 or more than $13? Explain.

_____

_____

6. Is there any price for which no shirts were sold? Explain.

_____

_____

Measure Length

Measure the length to the nearest half inch.

1.

_____ inches

2.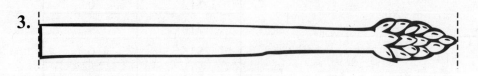

_____ inches

3.

_____ inches

Measure the length to the nearest fourth inch.

4.

_____ inches

5.

_____ inches

6.

_____ inch

7.

_____ inches

PROBLEM SOLVING

8. Draw 8 lines that are between 1 inch and 3 inches long on a separate sheet of paper. Measure each line to the nearest fourth inch and make a line plot.

_____

9. The tail on Alex's dog is $5\frac{1}{4}$ inches long. This length is between which two inch-marks on a ruler?

_____

Estimate and Measure Liquid Volume

Estimate how much liquid volume there will be when the container is filled.
Write *more than 1 liter*, *about 1 liter*, or *less than 1 liter*.

1. large milk container

_____

2. small milk container

_____

3. large water bottle

_____

4. spoonful of water

_____

5. bathtub filled halfway

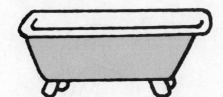

_____

6. filled eyedropper

_____

PROBLEM SOLVING

Use the pictures for 7–8. Alan pours water
into four glasses that are the same size.

7. Which glass has the most water?

_____

8. Which glass has the least water?

_____

A   B   C   D

Kilograms

Read each scale and write the weight. Then circle the better estimate.

1.

_____ kilogram

more than 1 kilogram

less than 1 kilogram

more than 1 kilogram

less than 1 kilogram

2.

_____ kilograms

more than 5 kilograms

less than 5 kilograms

more than 5 kilograms

less than 5 kilograms

LOGICAL REASONING

Circle the better estimate.

3. About how much does a brick weigh?

   2 kilograms   20 kilograms

4. About how much does a storybook weigh?

   1 kilogram   10 kilograms

5. About how much does a pony weigh?

   3 kilograms   300 kilograms

6. About how much does a watermelon weigh?

   2 kilograms   200 kilograms

Exploring Weight: Gram and Kilogram

Which unit of measure would you use to weigh each item? Write *gram* or *kilogram*.

 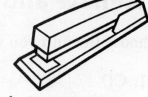

1. an envelope

2. a crayon

3. a desk

_____   _____   _____

Complete each sentence. Write *grams* or *kilograms*.

4. Vic's dog weighs about 10 _____.

5. The dog's bone weighs about 65 _____.

Use the graph for Exercises 6–8.

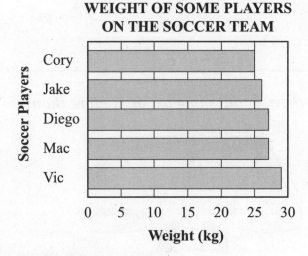

WEIGHT OF SOME PLAYERS ON THE SOCCER TEAM

6. Which student weighs the most?

_____

7. Which students are the same weight?

_____

8. Write Cory's and Jake's weight.

_____

MIXED REVIEW

Use the clues to name each figure.

9. I have 4 sides and 4 corners. All of my sides are the same length. All of my corners are the same size. What am I?

_____

10. I am a flat shape. I have 0 straight sides and 0 corners. I am round. What am I?

_____

11. I have 3 sides and 3 corners. Sometimes my corners are the same size, but sometimes they are different. What am I?

_____

12. I am a rectangle. If you draw a line from one of my corners to the opposite corner, you make 2 shapes. What are the 2 shapes?

_____

Name _____ Date _____

Estimate and Measure Mass

Choose the unit you would use to measure the mass. Write *gram* or *kilogram*.

1. CD

2. boy

3. bag of sugar

_____

_____

_____

4. lion

5. paper clip

6. empty plastic bottle

_____

_____

_____

Compare the masses of the objects. Write *is less than, is the same as,* or *is more than.*

7.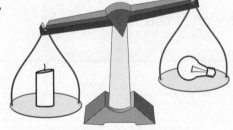

The mass of the candle _____ the mass of the light bulb.

8.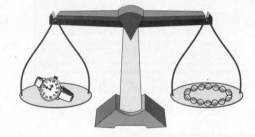

The mass of the watch _____ the mass of the necklace.

PROBLEM SOLVING

9. A red ball has a mass that is less than 1 kilogram. A blue ball has a mass of 1 kilogram. Is the mass of the blue ball more than or less than the mass of the red ball?

_____

10. Brock's dog is a collie. To find the mass of his dog, should Brock use *grams* or *kilograms*?

_____

Solve Problems About Liquid Volume and Mass

Write an equation and solve the problem.

1. Luis was served 145 grams of meat and 217 grams of vegetables at a meal. What was the total mass of the meat and the vegetables?

   Think: Add to find how much in all.

   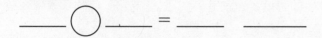

2. The gas tank of a riding mower holds 5 liters of gas. How many 5-liter gas tanks can you fill from a full 20-liter gas can?

3. To make a lemon-lime drink, Mac mixed 4 liters of lemonade with 2 liters of limeade. How much lemon-lime drink did Mac make?

   _____ ◯ _____ = _____ _____

4. A nickel has a mass of 5 grams. There are 40 nickels in a roll of nickels. What is the mass of a roll of nickels?

5. Four families share a basket of 16 kilograms of apples equally. How many kilograms of apples does each family get?

   _____ ◯ _____ = _____ _____

6. For a party, Julia made 12 liters of fruit punch. There were 3 liters of fruit punch left after the party. How much fruit punch did the people drink at the party?

   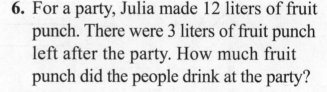

PROBLEM SOLVING

7. Zoe's fish tank holds 27 liters of water. She uses a 3-liter container to fill the tank. How many times does she have to fill the 3-liter container in order to fill her fish tank?

   _____

8. Adrian's backpack has a mass of 15 kilograms. Theresa's backpack has a mass of 8 kilograms. What is the total mass of both backpacks?

   _____

Thirds

Circle the fraction that each shape shows.

1.

$\frac{1}{2}$ $\frac{1}{3}$ $\frac{1}{2}$ $\frac{1}{3}$ $\frac{1}{2}$ $\frac{1}{3}$

2.

$\frac{1}{2}$ $\frac{1}{3}$ $\frac{1}{2}$ $\frac{1}{3}$ $\frac{1}{2}$ $\frac{1}{3}$

Find the shapes that show three equal parts. Color $\frac{1}{3}$.

3.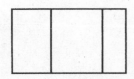

4.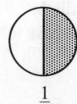

VISUAL THINKING

5. Which is greater, $\frac{1}{2}$ or $\frac{1}{3}$?
   Circle the greater fraction.

$\frac{1}{2}$ $\frac{1}{3}$

Visualize the Results

What is missing from each circle on the right?
Find the missing part. Draw lines to match.

1. $\frac{1}{2}$ •   •

2. $\frac{1}{3}$ •   •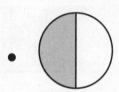

3. $\frac{1}{4}$ •   •

How does the rest of each picture look? Draw the missing part to complete.

4.

$\frac{1}{2}$ triangle

5.

$\frac{1}{3}$ pie

NUMBER SENSE

6. There were 3 fair shares.
Circle the fraction that tells what
part of the pizza has been eaten.

$\frac{1}{2}$ $\frac{2}{3}$

Exploring Fractions

Write the fraction for the part that is shaded. Then say the fraction.

1.   ⬜ shaded parts / ⬜ parts in all

2. 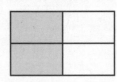 ⬜ shaded parts / ⬜ parts in all

3.   ⬜ / ⬜

4.   ⬜ / ⬜

5.   ⬜ / ⬜

Write the fraction for the part that is shaded.

6. 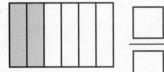 ⬜ / ⬜

7. 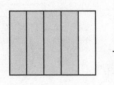 ⬜ / ⬜

8. 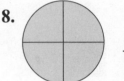 ⬜ / ⬜

Write the fraction for each word name.

9. one third ⬜ / ⬜

10. two fifths ⬜ / ⬜

11. four sixths ⬜ / ⬜

EVERYDAY MATH CONNECTION

Many foods must be divided into fraction parts in order for people to share them. Shade one fourth of each food item to show one serving out of four.

12.

13.

14.

Name _____ Date _____

Part of a Whole and Part of a Group

Write *part of a whole* or *part of a group* to describe each example.

1.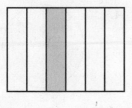

$\frac{1}{6}$ _____

2.

$\frac{3}{4}$ _____

3.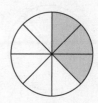

$\frac{3}{8}$ _____

4. Circle the figures that show thirds.

 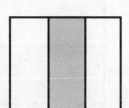  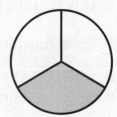

Write the words that name each fraction.

5. $\frac{1}{2}$

_____

_____

_____

6. $\frac{1}{8}$

_____

_____

_____

7. $\frac{3}{4}$

_____

_____

_____

LOGICAL REASONING

8. Christina folds a piece of paper in half. Then she folds it in half again. When she unfolds the paper, how many boxes does it show? _____

9. Christina colors one of the boxes. What fraction does it show? _____

10. A piece of paper was folded in half many times. When opened up it showed 16 boxes. How many times was the paper folded? _____

Part of a Whole

Write a fraction for the shaded part.

1.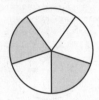

2.

3.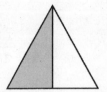

4.

_____   _____   _____   _____

Use this rectangle to answer Exercises 5–7.

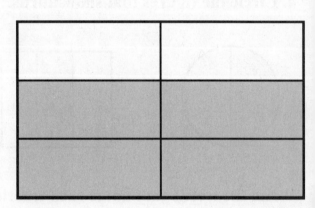

5. How much of the figure is shaded? _____

6. How much of the figure is not shaded? _____

7. How many sixths are in 1 whole? _____

MIXED APPLICATIONS

8. Ben cut a pizza into 8 equal pieces. He ate 3 pieces. What fraction of the pizza was left?

9. Ben cut 8 mushrooms to put on his pizza. He cut each mushroom into 4 pieces. How many pieces of mushroom are on the pizza?

_____   _____

Understanding Part of a Group

Color to show the fractions.

1.

$\frac{1}{3}$ green, $\frac{2}{3}$ yellow

2.

$\frac{2}{3}$ orange, $\frac{1}{3}$ red

3.

$\frac{2}{5}$ blue, $\frac{3}{5}$ orange

4.

$\frac{4}{5}$ purple, $\frac{1}{5}$ yellow

5.

$\frac{3}{4}$ green, $\frac{1}{4}$ purple

6.

$\frac{2}{4}$ yellow, $\frac{2}{4}$ red

7.

$\frac{4}{6}$ red, $\frac{2}{6}$ blue

8.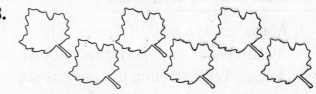

$\frac{3}{6}$ green, $\frac{3}{6}$ purple

PROBLEM SOLVING

Write the answer.

9. There are 4 trees. $\frac{1}{4}$ of the trees are yellow. The rest are orange. How many trees are orange?

10. What fraction of the trees are orange?

_____   _____

123

Naming Part of a Group

Write the fraction.

1.

What fraction are white? _____

2.

What part is white? _____

3.

What part is shaded? _____

4.

What part is shaded? _____

5. None of the five girls played volleyball. _____

6. All of the nine teachers watched the game. _____

MIXED APPLICATIONS

7. Maria needs a total of 4 eggs in her muffin batter. She has already added 3 eggs. What fraction of eggs has she already added to the batter?

_____

8. Maria gathers 398 red apples, 179 green apples, and 159 golden apples from her apple orchards. She wants to put 800 apples for sale in her store. How many more does she need to gather?

_____

EVERYDAY MATH CONNECTION

9. How many dimes does it take to equal one dollar? _____

10. What fraction of a dollar is represented by one dime? _____

124

Fractions on a Number Line

Use fraction strips to help you complete the number line.
Then locate and draw a point for the fraction.

1. $\frac{1}{3}$

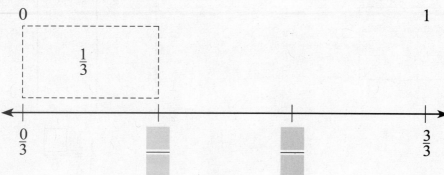

2. $\frac{3}{4}$

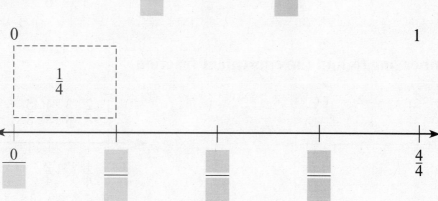

Write the fraction that names the points.

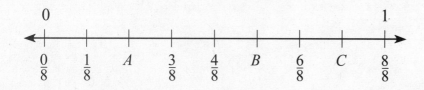

3. point A _____

4. point B _____

5. point C _____

PROBLEM SOLVING

Write the answer.

6. Jade ran 6 times around her neighborhood to complete a total of 1 mile. How many times will she need to run to complete $\frac{5}{6}$ of a mile?

7. A missing fraction on a number line is located exactly halfway between $\frac{3}{6}$ and $\frac{5}{6}$. What is the missing fraction?

_____

_____

125

Model Equivalent Fractions

Shade the model. Then divide the pieces to find the equivalent fraction.

1.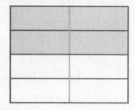

$\dfrac{2}{4} = \dfrac{\square}{8}$

2.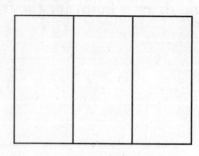

$\dfrac{1}{3} = \dfrac{\square}{6}$

Use the number line to find the equivalent fraction.

3.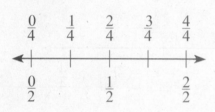

$\dfrac{1}{2} = \dfrac{\square}{4}$

4.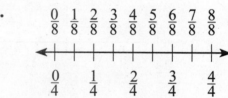

$\dfrac{3}{4} = \dfrac{\square}{8}$

PROBLEM SOLVING

5. Mike says that $\frac{3}{3}$ of his fraction model is shaded blue. Ryan says that $\frac{6}{6}$ of the same model is shaded blue. Are the two fractions equivalent? If so, what is another equivalent fraction?

_____

6. Brett shaded $\frac{4}{8}$ of a sheet of notebook paper. Aisha says he shaded $\frac{1}{2}$ of the paper. Are the two fractions equivalent? If so, what is another equivalent fraction?

_____

Recognize Equivalent Fractions

Write *true* or *false*.

1.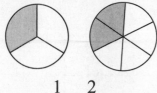

$$\frac{1}{3} = \frac{2}{6}$$

_____

2.

$$\frac{1}{2} = \frac{1}{3}$$

_____

3.

$$\frac{1}{2} = \frac{2}{4}$$

_____

4.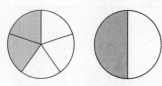

$$\frac{3}{5} = \frac{1}{2}$$

_____

5.

$$\frac{2}{3} = \frac{4}{6}$$

_____

6.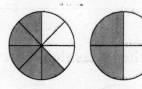

$$\frac{5}{8} = \frac{2}{4}$$

_____

Name the equivalent fraction that is shown.

7.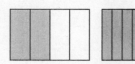

$$\frac{2}{4} = \frac{\square}{8}$$

8.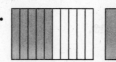

$$\frac{5}{10} = \frac{\square}{2}$$

9.

$$\frac{2}{5} = \frac{\square}{10}$$

10.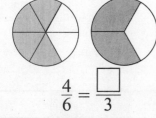

$$\frac{4}{6} = \frac{\square}{3}$$

11.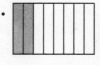

$$\frac{2}{8} = \frac{\square}{4}$$

12.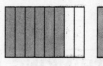

$$\frac{6}{8} = \frac{\square}{4}$$

MIXED REVIEW

Find the product or quotient.

13. $\begin{array}{r} 5 \\ \times\,3 \\ \hline \end{array}$

14. $\begin{array}{r} 8 \\ \times\,5 \\ \hline \end{array}$

15. $\begin{array}{r} 7 \\ \times\,7 \\ \hline \end{array}$

16. $\begin{array}{r} 4 \\ \times\,9 \\ \hline \end{array}$

17. $\begin{array}{r} 9 \\ \times\,6 \\ \hline \end{array}$

18. $\begin{array}{r} 0 \\ \times\,2 \\ \hline \end{array}$

19. $4\overline{)32}$

20. $5\overline{)45}$

21. $4\overline{)28}$

22. $8\overline{)48}$

23. $6\overline{)36}$

Exploring Equivalent Fractions

Write the fraction for the shaded part. Make a model and fold it in half from top to bottom. Write the new fraction.

1.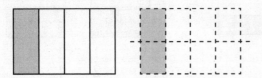

_____

2.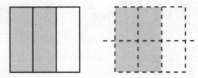

_____

Write the equivalent fractions for each pair of pictures.

3.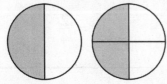

_____

4.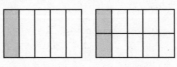

_____

5.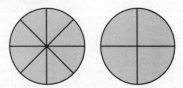

_____

Draw pictures to show equivalent fractions.

6. $\frac{4}{8} = \frac{1}{2}$

7. $\frac{6}{10} = \frac{3}{5}$

VISUAL THINKING

8. Compare these fractions. What happens when you multiply the numerator and the denominator by the same number?

$\frac{2}{3}$

$\frac{4}{6}$

$\frac{6}{9}$

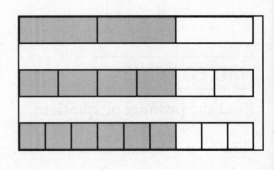

Name _____ Date _____

Find Equivalent Fractions

Use the pictures to find the missing numerator or denominator.

1. $\dfrac{1}{3} = \dfrac{3}{\boxed{}}$

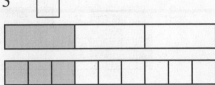

2. $\dfrac{\boxed{}}{4} = \dfrac{6}{8}$

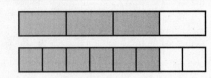

Circle the fractions that are equivalent to the given fraction.
Draw pictures if you need to.

3. $\dfrac{1}{3}$ $\dfrac{2}{6}$ $\dfrac{3}{9}$ $\dfrac{4}{10}$ $\dfrac{1}{2}$

4. $\dfrac{1}{4}$ $\dfrac{3}{6}$ $\dfrac{2}{8}$ $\dfrac{1}{2}$ $\dfrac{3}{12}$

5. $\dfrac{1}{2}$ $\dfrac{4}{8}$ $\dfrac{6}{6}$ $\dfrac{2}{4}$ $\dfrac{3}{5}$

MIXED APPLICATIONS

Use the graphs for Exercises 6–8.

6. How many more red balls does Heather have than Tom?

_____

7. Write a fraction to show what part of Heather's balls are red.

_____

8. Write two equivalent fractions to show what part of Tom's bag has green balls.

_____

Heather's Bag

Tom's Bag

VISUAL THINKING

9. Use the graphs in Exercises 6–8. Write a problem using fractions. Solve.

_____

129

Simplest Form

Use a picture to find the simplest form of each fraction.
The simplest form has the fewest parts.

1.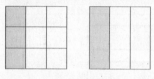

$$\frac{3}{9} = \frac{\Box}{3}$$

2.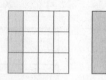

$$\frac{3}{12} = \frac{\Box}{4}$$

3.

$$\frac{8}{10} = \frac{\Box}{5}$$

Use division to find the simplest form of each fraction.

4. $\dfrac{10}{12} = \dfrac{10 \div 2}{12 \div 2} = \dfrac{\Box}{\Box}$

5. $\dfrac{6}{9} = \dfrac{6 \div 3}{9 \div 3} = \dfrac{\Box}{\Box}$

6. $\dfrac{4}{12} = \dfrac{4 \div 4}{12 \div 4} = \dfrac{\Box}{\Box}$

Write each fraction in simplest form.

7. $\dfrac{2}{14}$ _____

8. $\dfrac{3}{18}$ _____

9. $\dfrac{5}{10}$ _____

10. $\dfrac{3}{9}$ _____

MIXED APPLICATIONS

Write the time and A.M. or P.M.

11. Brian goes to school at $\frac{1}{4}$ hour past 8:00. What time does Brian go to school?

_____

12. Brian has dinner at $\frac{1}{2}$ hour past 5:00. What time does Brian have dinner?

_____

Relate Fractions and Whole Numbers

**Use the number line to find whether the
two numbers are equal. Write *equal* or *not equal*.**

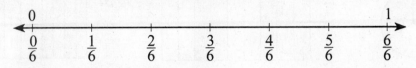

1. $\frac{0}{6}$ and 1

2. 1 and $\frac{6}{6}$

3. $\frac{1}{6}$ and $\frac{6}{6}$

_____   _____   _____

Each shape is 1 whole. Write a fraction for the parts that are shaded.

4. 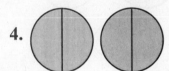   2 = _____

5.   4 = _____

6.    3 = _____

7. 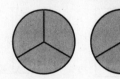   1 = _____

PROBLEM SOLVING

8. Rachel jogged along a trail that was $\frac{1}{4}$ of a mile long. She jogged along the trail 8 times. How many miles did Rachel jog in all?

_____

9. Jon ran around a track that was $\frac{1}{8}$ of a mile long. He ran around the track 24 times. How many miles did Jon run in all?

_____

Name _____ Date _____

Exploring Comparing Fractions

Compare. Write < or > in each ◯.

1.
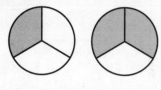

$\frac{1}{3}$ ◯ $\frac{2}{3}$

2.
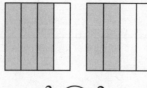

$\frac{3}{4}$ ◯ $\frac{2}{4}$

3.
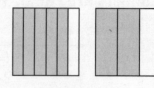

$\frac{5}{6}$ ◯ $\frac{2}{3}$

Compare. Write <, >, or = in each ◯.

4.
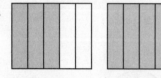

$\frac{3}{4}$ ◯ $\frac{4}{5}$

5.
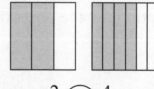

$\frac{2}{3}$ ◯ $\frac{4}{6}$

6.
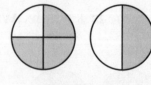

$\frac{3}{4}$ ◯ $\frac{1}{2}$

7.
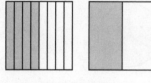

$\frac{4}{8}$ ◯ $\frac{1}{2}$

8.
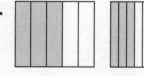

$\frac{3}{5}$ ◯ $\frac{3}{8}$

9.
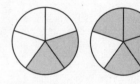

$\frac{2}{5}$ ◯ $\frac{4}{5}$

Solve.

10. Quint has finished $\frac{2}{5}$ of his math homework. Greta has completed $\frac{2}{3}$ of the same homework. Who has completed more?

_____

11. A bowl of muffin batter contains $\frac{1}{3}$ cup of oil and $\frac{2}{3}$ cup of milk. Do the muffins have more milk or more oil?

_____

WRITER'S CORNER

12. Two pizzas are equal in size. One is cut into 6 equal pieces. The other is cut into 8 equal pieces. Which pizza has larger pieces? Explain your answer.

_____

_____

132

Name _____ Date _____

Compare Fractions with the Same Denominator

Compare. Write <, >, or = .

1. $\frac{3}{4}$ ◯ $\frac{1}{4}$ 2. $\frac{3}{6}$ ◯ $\frac{0}{6}$ 3. $\frac{1}{2}$ ◯ $\frac{1}{2}$

4. $\frac{5}{6}$ ◯ $\frac{6}{6}$ 5. $\frac{7}{8}$ ◯ $\frac{5}{8}$ 6. $\frac{2}{3}$ ◯ $\frac{3}{3}$

7. $\frac{8}{8}$ ◯ $\frac{0}{8}$ 8. $\frac{1}{6}$ ◯ $\frac{1}{6}$ 9. $\frac{3}{4}$ ◯ $\frac{2}{4}$

10. $\frac{1}{6}$ ◯ $\frac{2}{6}$ 11. $\frac{1}{2}$ ◯ $\frac{0}{2}$ 12. $\frac{3}{8}$ ◯ $\frac{3}{8}$

13. $\frac{1}{4}$ ◯ $\frac{4}{4}$ 14. $\frac{5}{8}$ ◯ $\frac{4}{8}$ 15. $\frac{4}{6}$ ◯ $\frac{6}{6}$

PROBLEM SOLVING

16. Ben mowed $\frac{5}{6}$ of his lawn in one hour. John mowed $\frac{4}{6}$ of his lawn in one hour. Who mowed less of his lawn in one hour?

17. Darcy baked 8 muffins. She put blueberries in $\frac{5}{8}$ of the muffins. She put raspberries in $\frac{3}{8}$ of the muffins. Did more muffins have blueberries or raspberries?

_____   _____

133

Compare Fractions with the Same Numerator

Compare. Write $<$, $>$, or $=$.

1. $\frac{1}{8}$ ◯ $\frac{1}{2}$

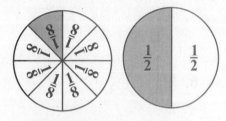

2. $\frac{3}{8}$ ◯ $\frac{3}{6}$

3. $\frac{2}{3}$ ◯ $\frac{2}{4}$

4. $\frac{2}{8}$ ◯ $\frac{2}{3}$

5. $\frac{3}{6}$ ◯ $\frac{3}{4}$

6. $\frac{1}{2}$ ◯ $\frac{1}{6}$

7. $\frac{5}{6}$ ◯ $\frac{5}{8}$

8. $\frac{4}{8}$ ◯ $\frac{4}{8}$

9. $\frac{6}{8}$ ◯ $\frac{6}{6}$

PROBLEM SOLVING

10. Javier is buying food in the lunch line. The tray of salad plates is $\frac{3}{8}$ full. The tray of fruit plates is $\frac{3}{4}$ full. Which tray is more full?

_____

11. Rachel bought some buttons. Of the buttons, $\frac{2}{4}$ are yellow and $\frac{2}{8}$ are red. Rachel bought more of which color buttons?

_____

Compare and Order Fractions

Write the fractions in order from greatest to least.

1. $\frac{4}{4}, \frac{1}{4}, \frac{3}{4}$ _____, _____, _____

    Think: The denominators
    are the same, so compare
    the numerators: $4 > 3 > 1$.

2. $\frac{2}{8}, \frac{5}{8}, \frac{1}{8}$ _____, _____, _____

3. $\frac{1}{3}, \frac{1}{6}, \frac{1}{2}$ _____, _____, _____

4. $\frac{2}{3}, \frac{2}{6}, \frac{2}{8}$ _____, _____, _____

Write the fractions in order from least to greatest.

5. $\frac{2}{4}, \frac{4}{4}, \frac{3}{4}$ _____, _____, _____

6. $\frac{4}{6}, \frac{5}{6}, \frac{2}{6}$ _____, _____, _____

7. $\frac{7}{8}, \frac{0}{8}, \frac{3}{8}$ _____, _____, _____

8. $\frac{3}{4}, \frac{3}{6}, \frac{3}{8}$ _____, _____, _____

PROBLEM SOLVING

9. Mr. Jackson ran $\frac{7}{8}$ mile on Monday. He ran $\frac{3}{8}$ mile on Wednesday and $\frac{5}{8}$ mile on Friday. On which day did Mr. Jackson run the shortest distance?

   _____

10. Delia has three pieces of ribbon. Her red ribbon is $\frac{2}{4}$ foot long. Her green ribbon is $\frac{2}{3}$ foot long. Her yellow ribbon is $\frac{2}{6}$ foot long. She wants to use the longest piece for a project. Which color ribbon should Delia use?

   _____

Unit 13
Core Skills Math, Grade 3

Exploring Estimation: Rounding

Round to the nearest ten cents or the nearest ten.

1. 43 _____

2. 79 _____

3. 89 _____

4. 61 _____

5. 33¢ _____

6. 47¢ _____

7. 62¢ _____

8. 85¢ _____

9. 54 _____

10. 58¢ _____

11. 19 _____

12. 45¢ _____

Write the numbers in each row that round to the number in the box.

13. 85   83   78   75   88   80   _____

14. 63¢   71¢   65¢   67¢   69¢   70¢   _____

15. Write the numbers that round to 10.

_____

16. Kathy estimates that she saw about 50 geese at the pond. What is the least number of geese she may have seen? the greatest number?

_____

17. Kathy's suitcase weighs between 20 and 30 pounds. She thinks it weighs closer to 20 pounds. What could the weight of her suitcase be?

_____

CONSUMER CONNECTION

18. You are told that you can spend about 50¢ at the toy store. Circle the items you can choose from.

Name _____ Date _____

Rounding to the Nearest Hundred

Use the number line. Round each number to the nearest hundred.

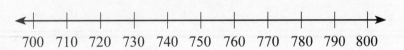

700 710 720 730 740 750 760 770 780 790 800

1. 785 _____   **2.** 742 _____   **3.** 719 _____   **4.** 752 _____

Round each number to the nearest hundred.

5. 587 _____   **6.** 279 _____   **7.** 848 _____   **8.** 920 _____

9. 328 _____   **10.** 489 _____   **11.** 176 _____   **12.** 512 _____

Write the number that is halfway between the two hundreds.

13. 300, 400 _____   **14.** 800, 900 _____   **15.** 600, 700 _____

MIXED APPLICATIONS

16. A jet crew is made up of 2 pilots, 8 flight attendants, and 1 flight supervisor. How many people are in the crew?

_____

17. The small jet carried 378 people from New York to Washington. To the nearest hundred, about how many people were on the flight?

_____

NUMBER SENSE

18. Does rounding to the nearest ten or rounding to the nearest hundred give a closer estimate? Explain.

Example
378
to the nearest ten—380
to the nearest hundred—400

_____

_____

_____

137

Round to the Nearest Ten or Hundred

Locate and label 739 on the number line. Round to the nearest hundred.

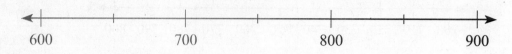

600   700   800   900

1. 739 is between _____ and _____.

2. 739 is closer to _____ than it is to _____.

3. 739 rounded to the nearest hundred is _____.

Round to the nearest ten and hundred.

4. 363 _____

        _____

5. 829 _____

        _____

6. 572 _____

        _____

7. 209 _____

        _____

8. 663 _____

        _____

9. 949 _____

        _____

10. 762 _____

        _____

11. 399 _____

        _____

12. 402 _____

        _____

PROBLEM SOLVING

13. The baby elephant weighs 435 pounds. What is its weight rounded to the nearest hundred pounds?

_____

14. Jayce sold 218 cups of lemonade at his lemonade stand. What is 218 rounded to the nearest ten?

_____

Name _____ Date _____

Choose a Strategy

Draw a picture or use counters to solve.

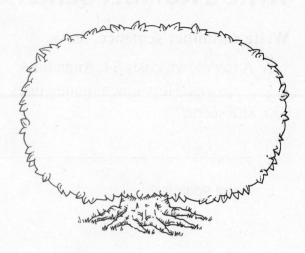

1. There are 12 oranges. There are 3 trees. Each tree has an equal number of oranges on it. How many oranges are on each tree?

   _____

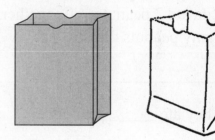

2. There are 4 ears of corn in the blue bag. There are twice as many ears of corn in the white bag. How many ears of corn are there in the bags?

   _____

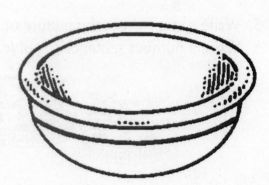

3. Lindy had 16 grapes. She ate half of them. How many grapes does Lindy have left?

   _____

NUMBER SENSE

Circle the better estimate.

4. There are 2 groups of 4 birds. One group flies away. How many birds are left?

   more than 8

   fewer than 8

Write a Number Sentence

Write a number sentence. Solve.

1. A toy clown costs $4. Anna buys
2 clowns. How much money does
she spend?

_____

Anna spends _____.

2. Owen draws 21 circus pictures. Julie
draws 16 pictures. How many more
pictures does Owen draw than Julie?

_____

Owen draws _____ more pictures.

3. Nancy ate 8 peanuts. Paul ate 9 peanuts.
Lita ate 7 peanuts. All together, how
many peanuts did they eat?

_____

They ate _____ peanuts.

4. Jay has 5 toy circus tents. He puts 4 toy
tigers in each. How many tigers are in
the tents?

_____

There are _____ toy tigers.

STORY CORNER

5. Write a story about the picture of circus clowns. Make up a problem.
Write a number sentence to solve it.

_____

_____

_____

Problem Solving

TWO-STEP PROBLEMS

Solve the problem.

1. Jack has 3 boxes of pencils with the same number of pencils in each box. His mother gives him 4 more pencils. Now Jack has 28 pencils. How many pencils are in each box?

   Think: I can start with 28 counters and act out the problem.

   _____

2. The art teacher has 48 paintbrushes. She puts 8 paintbrushes on each table in her classroom. How many tables are in her classroom?

   _____

3. Ricardo has 2 cases of video games with the same number of games in each case. He gives 4 games to his brother. Ricardo has 10 games left. How many video games were in each case?

   _____

4. Patty has $20 to spend on gifts for her friends. Her mother gives her $5 more. If each gift costs $5, how many gifts can she buy?

   _____

5. Joe has a collection of 35 DVD movies. He received 8 of them as gifts. Joe bought the rest of his movies over 3 years. If he bought the same number of movies each year, how many movies did Joe buy last year?

   _____

6. Liz has a 24-inch-long ribbon. She cuts nine 2-inch pieces from her original ribbon. How much of the original ribbon is left?

   _____

Guess and Check

Use guess and check to solve.

1. Earl is 8 years younger than Denise. The sum of their ages is 42. How old is each?

_____

2. What two numbers have a sum of 123 and a difference of 7?

_____

3. In all, planets A and B have 34 moons. Planet B has 2 more moons than Planet A. How many moons does each planet have?

_____

4. In a basketball game, Anita scored 37 points on 2-point and 3-point shots. She scored 6 more 2-pointers than 3-pointers. How many of each did she score?

_____

5. Sea otters and seals can stay underwater for a long time. Together, they can last 27 minutes without taking a breath. Seals can stay under 17 minutes longer than otters. How long can otters stay underwater?

_____

6. Sound is measured in decibels (dB). The sound of loud rock music is 30 dB less than the sound of a rocket taking off. Combined, the two sounds measure 230 dB. How loud is a rocket taking off?

_____

Name _____ Date _____

Choose an Operation

Choose an operation to solve. Write *addition, subtraction,*
multiplication, **or** *division.* **Then solve the problem.**

1. The Warren family left home and drove
   370 miles on the first day of vacation.
   They drove 76 miles on the second day.
   They still had 117 miles to go to get to
   their campground. How far was it from
   home to the campground?

   _____

   _____

2. Each member of a hiking club gave
   6 hours of service on Saturday. If
   they gave 54 hours in all, how many
   members were there?

   _____

   _____

3. Nolan Ryan had 5,714 career
   strikeouts. Steve Carlton had 4,136
   career strikeouts. How many more
   strikeouts did Nolan Ryan have than
   Steve Carlton?

   _____

   _____

4. There are 5 days of school during most
   weeks of a school year. How many days
   of school are there in 8 full weeks?

   _____

   _____

5. Halley's Comet returns to Earth every
   76 years. It was last seen in 1986. When
   should the comet return next?

   _____

   _____

6. Camels can drink about 420 pints of
   water in one hour. How much water can
   camels drink in 1 minute?

   Hint: 1 hour = 60 minutes

   _____

   _____

Answer Key

Page 1
1. 8
2. 11
3. 11
4. 12
5. 15
6. 11
7. 13
8. 14
9. 13
10. 11
11. 12
12. 10
13. 12
14. 12
15. 9
16. 11
17. 16
18. 10
19. 15
20. 10
21. 15 fish
22. 8 rainbow fish
23. bottom number line
24. top number line
25. middle number line

Page 2
1. 6
2. 15
3. 15
4. 13
5. 17
6. 5
7. 9
8. 10
9. 13
10. 11
11. 4
12. 15
13. 11
14. 12
15. 13
16. 11
17. 8
18. 17
19. 14
20. 14
21. 16
22. 13
23. 18

24. 16
25. 9
26. 14
27. 10
28. 12
29. 15
30. 12 ounces
31. 10 months old
32. Answers will vary. Possible answers: 6, 10, 4, 12, 8
33. Answers will vary. Possible answers: 15, 17, 13, 11, 9

Page 3
1. 3
2. 4
3. 4
4. 7
5. 2
6. 7
7. 1
8. 3
9. 3
10. 3
11. 5
12. 1
13. 1
14. 5
15. 2
16. 2
17. 7
18. 5
19. 2
20. 1
21. 5 kittens
22. 3 more cans
23. 5¢, 6¢, 4¢

Page 4
1. 11; 2 + 9 = 11
2. 13; 10 + 3 = 13
3. 17; 9 + 8 = 17
4. 11; 7 + 4 = 11
5. 13; 7 + 6 = 13
6. 4; 4 + 0 = 4
7. 9; 6 + 3 = 9
8. 12; 5 + 7 = 12
9. 15; 6 + 9 = 15
10. odd
11. even

12. odd
13. even
14. odd
15. even
16. 8 + 10 = 18
17. No; 6 + 8 = 14, an even number.

Page 5
1. 80
2. 100
3. 100
4. 90
5. 80
6. 40
7. 60
8. 30
9. 60
10. 50
11. 90
12. 60
13. 77
14. 81
15. 69
16. 68
17. 32
18. 69
19. 89
20. 79
21. 89
22. 89
23. 91
24. 79
25. 80 minutes
26. 27 pieces of fruit
27. George; $0.05

Page 6
1. 90
2. 100
3. 100
4. 100
5. 120
6. 140
7. 99
8. 149
9. 106
10. 119
11. 99
12. 119
13. 84
14. 118

15. 134
16. 78
17. 119
18. 139
19. 98
20. 78
21. 139
22. 58
23. 118
24. 65
25. 52 minutes
26. 174 fish
27. less than 56
28. greater than 50

Page 7
1. 100 − 30 = 70
2. 50 − 20 = 30
3. 80 − 40 = 40
4. 70 − 10 = 60
5. 24
6. 21
7. 18
8. 43
9. 60
10. 11
11. 56
12. 37
13. 68
14. 10
15. 28
16. 15
17. $38
18. 43¢ more
19. Answers will vary.

Page 8
1. 30
2. 40
3. 10
4. 30
5. 0
6. 30
7. 67; 67 + 23 = 90
8. 32; 32 + 18 = 50
9. 34; 34 + 46 = 80
10. 7; 7 + 63 = 70
11. 23; 23 + 17 = 40
12. 33; 33 + 27 = 60
13. 11; 11 + 19 = 30
14. 45; 45 + 45 = 90
15. 93 birds

16. 23 flamingos
17. 5 days

Page 9

1. 69
2. 119
3. 51
4. 65
5. 109
6. 32
7. 99
8. 17
9. 35
10. 146
11. 44
12. 119
13. balloon
14. banner
15. stuffed lion, circus visor
16. 2,256; 1,897; 980
17. Answers will vary.

Page 10

1. 677
2. 1,378
3. 724
4. 162
5. 407
6. 1,179
7. 894
8. 893
9. 1,099
10. 568
11. 277
12. 847
13. 492
14. 939
15. 839
16. 1, 3, 4, 7, 8, 11, 13
17. 5, 15
18. 2, 6, 9
19. 10, 12, 14
20. 492
21. 716

Page 11

1. 650; 15, 6
2. 930
3. 821
4. 737
5. 520
6. 849
7. 602
8. 1,016

9. 658
10. 202
11. 1,372
12. 800
13. 304

Page 12

1. 1,125
2. 967
3. 1,500
4. 1,031
5. 1,689
6. 959
7. 1,127
8. 893
9. 795
10. 1,067
11. 918
12. 897
13. 1,109
14. 1,233
15. 719
16. 1,212 rolls and bagels
17. 833 boxes
18. yes
19. 1,320 yards

Page 13

1. 113
2. 443
3. 210
4. 661
5. 322
6. 112
7. 534
8. 233
9. 411
10. 126
11. 222
12. 132
13. 403
14. 335
15. 304
16. 102 miles
17. 205 minutes
18. Circle second model.

Page 14

1. 217
2. 265
3. 327
4. 718
5. 602
6. 925

7. 537
8. 250
9. 355
10. 225
11. 528
12. 503
13. 117 miles
14. 872 people
Circle problems 15 and 18.
15. 598
16. 370
17. 461
18. 604
19. 429

Page 15

1. 183
2. 277
3. 363
4. 661
5. 81
6. 154
7. 761
8. 80
9. 486
10. 215
11. 792
12. 331 more miles
13. 712 miles
14. Answers will vary.

Page 16

1. 87
2. 581
3. 377
4. 537
5. 114
6. 190
7. 135
8. 265
9. 20
10. 344
11. 151
12. 97
13. 33 miles more
14. 495 miles
15. will vary; even, odd, even, odd

Page 17

1. 245; b
2. 451; b
3. 104; c
4. 574; a

5. 118; c
6. 23
7. 57
8. 60
9. 114
10. 634

Page 18

1. 96
2. 524
3. 512
4. 322
5. 12
6. 154
7. 108
8. 535
9. 418
10. 199
11. 500
12. 400
13. 200
14. 200
15. 104 more kilometers per hour
16. 311 more kilometers
17. 414; Drawings should show 6 hundreds, 9 tens, 13 ones and crossing out of 2 hundreds, 8 tens, and 9 ones.

Page 19

1. 217; 217 + 644 = 861
2. 426; 426 + 427 = 853
3. 544; 544 + 46 = 590
4. 603; 603 + 145 = 748
5. 547; 547 + 419 = 966
6. 260; 260 + 348 = 608
7. 269; 269 + 207 = 476
8. 394; 394 + 425 = 819
9. 117 miles
10. 672 people
11. 841; 568; 273

Page 20

1. 11:00
2. 3:00
3. 7:00
4. 10 minutes
5. 45 minutes
6. 30 minutes
7. 3:00
8. on the 9
9. 832

Answer Key
Core Skills Math, Grade 3

10. 526
11. 341
12. 1,058
13. 514

Page 21

1. 9:15, 1:45, 4:30
2. 10:15, 2:45, 5:30
3. 9:45, 2:15, 5:00
4. 9:30, 2:00, 4:45
5. 3:30
6. 3:15
7. 10:00, ten o'clock
8. 5:15, five-fifteen
9. 7:30, seven-thirty

Page 22

1. 10, 15, 20
2. 10, 15, 20, 25
3. 10, 15, 20
4. 10, 15, 20, 25, 30
5. 4:14
6. 7:39
7. 8:24

Check drawings for 8–10.

Page 23

1. 10:30
2. 12:30
3. 2 hours
4. 1 hour
5. 30 minutes
6. 1 hour
7. 30 minutes
8. same length
9. an hour

Page 24

1. 8:15, 8:20, 8:25, 8:30
2. 11:00, 11:01, 11:02, 11:03
3. 6:45, 6:46, 6:47, 6:48
4. 4:30
5. 5:00

Page 25

1. 10:15, ten-fifteen
2. 3:55, three fifty-five
3. 8:30, eight-thirty
4. bottom clock
5. top clock
6. 36 minutes
7. Jason made bread dough.
8. five-fifteen

Page 26

1. 6:30 A.M.
2. 11:00 P.M.
3. 12:15 P.M.
4. Answers may vary.
5. Answers may vary.
6. whale movie
7. 10:45 A.M.
8. 6:00
9. 1:00

Page 27

Circle all pairs of shoes for 1–4.

1. 6, 6, 6
2. 8, 8, 4, 8
3. 4, 4, 2, 4
4. 10, 10, 5, 10
5. $5 \times 5 = 25$; 25
6. $5 \times 3 = 15$; 15
7. Answers will vary.

Page 28

1. Circle groups of 3; 2, 6
2. Circle groups of 4; 2, 8
3. Circle groups of 4; 4, 16
4. Circle groups of 3; 5, 15
5. Colton
6. Sasha
7. 4 stacks of 5 umbrellas

Page 29

1. $2 \times 4 = 8$; $4 \times 2 = 8$
2. $5 \times 3 = 15$; $3 \times 5 = 15$
3. $4 \times 3 = 12$; $3 \times 4 = 12$
4. $3 \times 2 = 6$; $2 \times 3 = 6$
5. $4 \times 4 = 16$; $4 \times 4 = 16$
6. $2 \times 5 = 10$; $5 \times 2 = 10$
7. Answers will vary.

Page 30

1. $4 \times 3 = 12$
2. $3 \times 4 = 12$
3. $1 \times 5 = 5$
4. $5 \times 1 = 5$
5. $5 \times 3 = 15$
6. $3 \times 5 = 15$
7. $4 + 4 + 4$
8. $2 + 2 + 2 + 2 + 2$
9. Answers will vary.

Page 31

1. 12, 12
2. 9, 9
3. 10, 10
4. 20, 20
5. 6, 6
6. 16, 16
7. $2 \times 4 = 8$
8. $4 \times 1 = 4$

Page 32

1. $8 + 8 = 16$; $2 \times 8 = 16$ or $4 + 4 + 4 + 4 = 16$; $4 \times 4 = 16$
2. $6 + 6 + 6 = 18$; $3 \times 6 = 18$ or $9 + 9 = 18$; $2 \times 8 = 19$

Check drawings for 3–5.

6. 15 airplanes
7. $4 + 4 + 4 + 4 = 16$; $4 \times 4 = 16$
8. $5¢ + 5¢ + 5¢ = 15¢$; $3 \times 5¢ = 15¢$
9. $5¢ + 5¢ + 5¢ + 5¢ + 5¢ = 25¢$; $5 \times 5¢ = 25¢$

Page 33

1. 10
2. 12
3. 16
4. $4 \times 2 = 8$
5. $2 \times 7 = 14$
6. $2 \times 3 = 6$
7. 10
8. 18
9. 8
10. 14
11. 16
12. 12
13. $6 \times 2 = 12$ roses
14. $24 + 36 + 48 = 108$ flowers
15. Marco 10; Juana 20; Luci 17

Page 34

1. 24
2. 12
3. 18
4. $6 \times 2 = 12$
5. $3 \times 7 = 21$
6. $3 \times 5 = 15$
7. 6

8. 27
9. 24
10. 21
11. 15
12. 18
13. 15 footballs
14. 41 golf balls
15. Edward; José 30 photos; Edward 36 photos

Page 35

Check drawings for 1–3.

1. 32
2. 8
3. 28
4. 24
5. 27
6. 8
7. 28
8. 36
9. 21
10. 9
11. 24
12. 16
13. 20
14. 24 buttons
15. 25 buttons
16. 8
17. 12
18. 16

Page 36

Check drawings for 1–3.

1. 20
2. 15
3. 30
4. 40
5. 10
6. 35
7. 25
8. 45
9. 28
10. 5
11. 24
12. 36
13. 20
14. $+$
15. $\times$
16. $-$
17. $5 \times 5 = 25$; 25¢
18. 40¢, 60¢
19. 6
20. 5

146

Answer Key
Core Skills Math, Grade 3

Page 37

1. 0
2. 8
3. 0
4. 7
5. 0
6. 3
7. 9
8. 0
9. 0
10. 10
11. 0
12. 6
13. 0
14. 3
15. 0
16. 0
17. 1
18. 0
19. 5
20. 0
21. 4
22. 0
23. 0
24. 2
25. 8 stickers
26. 24 more scented stickers
27. 491
28. 337
29. 792
30. 726
31. 901

Page 38

1. $3 \times 3 = 9$
2. $2 \times 5 = 10$
3. $4 \times 5 = 20$
4. $2 \times 8 = 16$
5. $3 \times 5 = 15$
6. $4 \times 4 = 16$
7. $3 \times 3 = 9$; $4 \times 4 = 16$
8. 25, yes
9. 24, no
10. 4, yes
11. 30, no
12. 8, no
13. 1, yes
14. 593
15. 196
16. 755
17. 450
18. 769

19. 8; $4 \times 2 = 8$
20. 25; $5 \times 5 = 25$

Page 39

1. 54
2. 48
3. 30
4. 42
5. 18
6. 24
7. 36
8. 48
9. 30
10. 6
11. 32
12. 30
13. 12
14. 35
15. 42
16. 54
17. 48 DVDs
18. $17
19. 7
20. 6 and 6

Page 40

1. 63
2. 21
3. 14
4. 56
5. 42
6. 63
7. 35
8. 28
9. 56
10. 7
11. 14
12. 27
13. 16
14. 24
15. 36
16. 35
17. 18
18. 48
19. 49
20. 56
21. $10
22. 56 boats
23. 28 days
24. 364 days

Page 41

1. 0, 8, 16, 24, 32, 40, 48, 56, 64, 72
2. 56
3. 36
4. 64
5. 40
6. 63
7. 16
8. 24
9. 72
10. 32
11. 48
12. 24 toy rings
13. $3 more
14. 40
15. 64
16. 80
17. 200

Page 42

1. 27
2. 36
3. 9
4. 18
5. 63
6. 81
7. 45
8. 72
9. 72
10. 63
11. 36
12. 54
13. 0
14. 45
15. 28
16. 36
17. 48
18. 36
19. 18
20. 27
21. 9 years old
22. 63 years old
23. 1, 9, 9
24. 2, 18, 18
25. 3, 27, 27
26. 4, 36, 36

Page 43

1. 24
2. 54
3. 8
4. 24
5. 0

6. 9
7. 48
8. 81
9. 20
10. 18
11. 0
12. 72
13. 7
14. 42
15. 0
16. 36
17. 49
18. 18
19. $18
20. 7 guests
21. $4 \times 7 = 28$; $7 \times 4 = 28$
22. $3 \times 6 = 18$; $6 \times 3 = 18$

Page 44

1. 21
2. 10

Check drawings for 3–6.

3. 8
4. 16
5. 6
6. 16
7. 28 tables
8. 24 singers

Page 45

1. $2 \times 5 = 10$
2. $4 \times 3 = 12$
3. 12
4. 32
5. 6
6. 24
7. 16
8. 14
9. 20
10. 8
11. 18 pages
12. 28 players

Page 46

1. 24
2. 21
3. 12
4. 15
5. 3
6. 48
7. 27
8. 36

Answer Key

Core Skills Math, Grade 3

9. 12
10. 30
11. 6
12. 18
13. 60
14. 18
15. 42
16. 0
17. 54
18. 9
19. 30
20. 6
21. 12 hits
22. 30 muffins

Page 47

1. even
2. even
3. even
4. even
5. odd
6. odd
7. even

Possible answers are given for 8–10.

8. The ones digits repeat 0 and 5. Each number is 5 more.
9. All the products are even. The ones digit is always 0.
10. The products of 6 are the products of 3 doubled.
11. the row for 4
12. Yes; the products are all even, or there is an even and odd pattern.

Page 48

Possible descriptions are given for 1–4.

1. 24, 30; Add 6 muffins for each pan; multiply the number of pans by 6.
2. 20, 24; Add 4 wheels for each wagon; multiply the number of wagons by 4.
3. 21, 35; Add 7 flowers for each vase; multiply the number of vases by 7.

4. 16, 32; Add 8 legs for each spider; multiply the number of spiders by 8.
5. 40 cups
6. 24 pencils

Page 49

1. b
2. c
3. a
4. d
5. a
6. 35
7. 36
8. 42
9. 0
10. 4
11. 0
12. 24
13. 18
14. 0
15. $4 \times 0 = 0$
16. $4 \times 8 = 32$
17. first and third arrays

Page 50

1. 89
2. 0
3. 15
4. 7
5. 1
6. 0
7. 16
8. 321
9. 50
10. $854 \times 0 = 0$
11. $119 \times 1 = 119$
12. $32
13. $21
14. 21 cubes

Page 51

Check drawings for 1–2.

1. 60
2. 54
3. 60, 54, 60 + 54 = 114; 114
4. 30, 15, 30 + 15 = 45; 45
5. 80, 56, 80 + 56 = 136; 136
6. 20, 4, 20 + 4 = 24; 24

7. 90, 27, 90 + 27 = 117; 117
8. 40, 24, 40 + 24 = 64; 64
9. Order may vary: 1 × 12, 2 × 6, 3 × 4, 4 × 3, 6 × 2, 12 × 1

Page 52

1. 180 spelling tests
2. 350 minutes
3. 100 tiles
4. 180 pairs of shoes
5. 320 students

Page 53

1. 80
2. 120
3. 7, 35, 350
4. 6, 24, 240
5. 3, 21, 210
6. 9, 27, 270
7. 250 gallons
8. 280 fish

Page 54

1. 200
2. 180
3. 300
4. 240
5. 100
6. 420
7. 280
8. 540
9. 630
10. 720
11. 480
12. $120
13. 350 minutes

Page 55

1. 60
2. 72
3. 48
4. 74
5. 39
6. 75
7. 56
8. 96
9. 64
10. 86
11. 75
12. 72
13. 58

14. 124
15. 108 foam lunch trays
16. 54¢
17. 170
18. 140
19. 120

Page 56

1. 54
2. 54
3. 84
4. 76
5. 85
6. 76
7. 92
8. 68
9. 80
10. 88
11. 75
12. 36
13. 72
14. 84
15. 65
16. 52
17. 72
18. 80
19. 62 letters
20. 60 readings
21. $315
22. $270
23. $180
24. $405

Page 57

Check circles for 1–4.

1. 2
2. 1
3. 4
4. 5
5. no
6. yes
7. no

Page 58

Check circles for 1–4.

1. 5
2. 2
3. 3
4. 2
5. 8
6. 10

148

Page 59

Check drawings for 1–4.
1. 3 fishbowls
2. 3 sofas
3. 5 boxes
4. putting 4 stickers on each page

Page 60

1. 6, 2, 3, 3
2. 21, 3, 7, 7
3. 12, 3, 4, 4
4. 3
5. 2
6. 5
7. 7
8. 4, 2
9. 9, 3
10. 16, 4

Page 61

1. 21, 3
2. 20, 5
3. $4 \times 6 = 24$;
   $6 \times 4 = 24$;
   $24 \div 4 = 6$;
   $24 \div 6 = 4$
4. $2 \times 5 = 10$;
   $5 \times 2 = 10$;
   $10 \div 2 = 5$;
   $10 \div 5 = 2$
5. $3 \times 9 = 27$;
   $9 \times 3 = 27$;
   $27 \div 3 = 9$;
   $27 \div 9 = 3$
6. Drawings should show 6 groups of 3.
7. 24 crayons
8. 2
9. 3
10. 6
11. 5

Page 62

Order may vary for 1–5.
1. $3 \times 4 = 12$;
   $12 \div 3 = 4$
2. $3 \times 6 = 18$;
   $18 \div 3 = 6$
3. 9, $9 \times 4 = 36$
4. 7, $35 \div 5 = 7$
5. 8, $72 \div 9 = 8$
6. Circle $8 \div 2$; 4 pots
7. 32

8. 72
9. 36

Page 63

1. 6
2. 5
3. 3
4. 6
5. 2
6. 4
7. 2
8. 8
9. 9
10. 1
11. 7
12. $6
13. 6
14. 24
15. 63
16. 32
17. 45
18. 56
19. 24
20. 5:15
21. 10:45

Page 64

1. $12 \div 3 = 4$ or
   $12 \div 4 = 3$
2. $18 \div 3 = 6$ or
   $18 \div 6 = 3$
3. 4
4. 6
5. 7
6. 4
7. 9
8. 8
9. 3
10. 2
11. $\div$
12. $\times$
13. $\div$
14. $\times$
15. 2:00
16. 285 cents
17. Drawings should show 2 diagonal lines crossing the center dot and 2 lines on each end to complete the squares.
18. Drawings should add one horizontal line that passes through the center.

Page 65

1. 6
2. 5
3. 6
4. 4
5. 7
6. 3
7. 5
8. 9
9. 8
10. 4
11. 8
12. 9
13. 3
14. 2
15. 3
16. 8
17. 6
18. 5
19. 7
20. 5
21. 7
22. 9
23. 8
24. 9
25. 4 students
26. 16 minutes
27. fewer
28. fewer

Page 66

1. 3
2. 4
3. 2
4. 6
5. 5
6. 3
7. 4
8. 5
9. 6
10. 6
11. 7
12. 9
13. 7
14. 6
15. 7
16. 8
17. 5
18. 5
19. 5
20. 8
21. 6
22. 6

23. 9
24. 1
25. 4
26. 4
27. 40 strands
28. 5 necklaces
29. 2 quarters
30. 5 quarters
31. 15 nickels
32. 40 nickels

Page 67

1. 1
2. 0
3. 7
4. 5
5. 8
6. 0
7. 1
8. 0
9. 0
10. 4
11. 5
12. 1
13. 6
14. 1
15. 9
16. 1
17. 35 minutes
18. 32 jars
19. 105 pieces
20. 4 pounds
21. 4
22. 3
23. 5
24. 4
25. 4
26. 3

Page 68

1. 4
2. 4
3. 5
4. 3
5. 4
6. 6
7. 4
8. 6
9. 5
10. 3
11. 3
12. 4
13. 4
14. 3

Answer Key
Core Skills Math, Grade 3

20. 802, 840, 885
21. 32 cartons
22. 8:20 A.M.
23. 6:30 P.M.
24. 4 × 3 = 12,
    3 × 4 = 12,
    12 ÷ 4 = 3,
    12 ÷ 3 = 4

Page 69

1. 3
2. 9
3. 1
4. 2
5. 4
6. 6
7. 9
8. 7
9. 8
10. 0
11. 5
12. 7
13. 4
14. 1
15. 3
16. 5
17. 9
18. 0
19. 2
20. 8
21. 9
22. 8
23. 6
24. 6
25. 6
26. 7
27. 8
28. 8
29. 7
30. 7
31. quotient 6, divisor 3
32. 4 kittens
33. a, 12¢

Page 70

1. 2
2. 4
3. 1
4. 7

5. 6
6. 3
7. 9
8. 8
9. 5
10. 2
11. 7
12. 4
13. 9
14. 8
15. 3
16. 6
17. 0
18. 4
19. 9
20. 1
21. ×
22. ÷
23. ÷
24. ÷
25. 999 plants
26. 7 mums
27. 4 hours
28. 7 hours

Page 71

1. 8
2. 0
3. 7
4. 6
5. 7
6. 3
7. 5
8. 9
9. 2
10. 0
11. 3
12. 4
13. 8
14. 6
15. 7
16. 1
17. 9
18. 6
19. 8
20. 9
21. 9
22. 8
23. 9 problems
24. 27 < 28; more
    subtraction problems
25. 827
26. 933
27. 147

28. 412
29. 244

Page 72

1. 6
2. 4
3. 9
4. 9
5. 2
6. 9
7. 8
8. 3
9. 4
10. 6
11. 9
12. 9
13. 1
14. 8
15. 6
16. 5
17. 0
18. 7
19. 9
20. 3
21. 9 students
22. $45
23. 6 and 8
24. Jon 2 runs, Kristi 6 runs
25. Answers will vary.

Page 73

1. 3
2. 6
3. 2
4. 5
5. 6
6. 6
7. 9
8. 9
9. 7
10. 6
11. 1
12. 9
13. 4
14. 7
15. 2
16. 1
17. 6
18. 7
19. 0
20. 2
21. 8
22. 2
23. 8

24. 7
25. 6
26. 9
27. 2
28. 7
29. 5
30. 5
31. 5
32. 0
33. 3
34. 3
35. 7 vans
36. $42

Page 74

1. 8 dinosaurs
2. 4 blocks
3. 2 cars
4. 9 crayons
5. Adam
6. Susan
7. 2, 4, 8
8. no

Page 75

1. 3 jump ropes
2. 9 pages
3. 7 crayons
4. 8 cards
5. 4 stickers

Page 76

1. 4
2. 8
3. 3
4. 9
5. 2
6. 7
7. 7
8. 9
9. 3
10. 6
11. 6
12. 5
13. 9
14. 8
15. 10
16. 6
17. $7
18. 6 muffins

Page 77

1. 4, 4
2. 9, 9

Answer Key

Core Skills Math, Grade 3

3. 1, 1
4. 9, 9
5. 3
6. 5
7. 7
8. 7
9. 8
10. 4
11. 2
12. 6
13. 2
14. 5
15. 8
16. 80
17. 8 adults
18. 4 tickets

Page 78

1. 4, 28, 52
2. 12, 18, 24
3. 20, 25, 35
4. 30, 50
5. yes
6. yes
7. no
8. yes
9. 3 students
10. 6 marbles
11. yes
12. yes
13. yes
14. no

Page 79

1. 2 ones, 2 tens, 2 hundreds
2. 4 ones, 4 tens, 4 hundreds
3. 2
4. 20
5. 200
6. 4
7. 40
8. 400
9. 6
10. 60
11. 600
12. 7
13. 70
14. 700
15. 200 books
16. 50 books

Page 80

1. circle
2. rectangle
3. triangle
4. pentagon
5. circle
6. square
7. square
8. rectangle
9. triangle
10. circle
11. pentagon
Answers will vary for 12–14.

Page 81

1. square, rectangle, rhombus
2. rectangle
3. trapezoid
4. B, D, and E
5. A and C
6. B, C, and D
7. square, rectangle, or rhombus
8. rhombus

Page 82

Check drawings for 1–3.
1. square or rhombus
2. trapezoid
3. Possible answer: I drew a trapezoid. It has only 1 pair of opposite sides that are parallel.
4. square, rhombus, or rectangle
5. rhombus

Page 83

1. B, 3
2. C, 0
3. A, 2
4. Kathy
5. 2 sides
6. 0 angles

Page 84

1. A; B and E; C and D
2. A, B, and C; D; none
3. A and D; B, C, and E; none

Page 85

Order of addends may vary for 1–3.
1. 6 + 5 + 4 = 15
2. 7 + 3 + 7 + 3 = 20
3. 3 + 5 + 6 + 8 = 22
4. 24

Page 86

Answers will vary for 1–7.
8. Possible answer: James can measure each side and add the lengths.

Page 87

Answers will vary for 1–6.
5. 10 + 10 + 4 + 4 = 28 cm
6. 2 + 2 + 2 + 2 + 2 + 2 + 2 = 16 cm
7. 36 in.
8. 52 cm
9. 180
10. 93
11. 24
12. 100
13. 87
14. 0
15. 1 hour

Page 88

1. 16 feet
2. 20 feet
3. 24 feet
4. 20 feet
5. 28 cm
6. 30 m
7. 104 inches

Page 89

1. 40 cm
2. 340 feet
3. 34 cm
4. 28 cm
5. 33 m
6. 28 cm
7. 60 inches
8. 8 inches

Page 90

Check drawings for 1–6.
1. 18 inches
2. 27 feet
3. 50 inches
4. 164 meters
5. 24 yards
6. 90 bricks

Page 91

Check drawings for 1–6.
1. 44 feet
2. 190 meters
3. 4,000 yards
4. 180 centimeters
5. 188 inches
6. 180 inches

Page 92

1. 6
2. 4
3. 5
4. 7
5. 8
6. 13
7. area
8. perimeter
9. 12 square units
10. 16 units

Page 93

1. 14
2. 16
3. 11
4. 22
5. 16 square meters
6. 19 square meters

Page 94

Answers will vary for 1–3. Check shapes for 6 square units.
4. 4 square units
5. 12 square units
6. 6 square units
7. 12 square units
8. 9 square units
9. 17 square units
10. 8 square units
11. 12 square units
12. 24 square units
13. Possible answers: I counted the units. I found the number of groups of 4 and multiplied that number by 4.

Page 95

1. 24 square feet
2. 16 square feet
3. 12 square meters
4. 24 square meters
5. 15 square meters
6. 20 square feet
7. 8 square inches

Page 96

1. 2; 2, 4; 4, 8; 16
2. For each mural, the width doubles and the length stays the same.
3. For each mural, the area doubles.
4. The areas are 25, 35, and 45 square feet. As the width increases, the areas increase by 10 square feet.

Page 97

Order of factors may vary for 1–6.
1. $5 \times 3 = 15$ square ft
2. $3 \times 3 = 9$ square ft
3. $10 \times 5 = 50$ square ft
4. $6 \times 8 = 48$ square feet
5. $6 \times 7 = 42$ square feet
6. $9 \times 5 = 45$ square feet
7. 72 square feet
8. 24 square feet
9. 54 square meters
10. 40 square centimeters
11. the rectangular poster

Page 98

Possible solution steps are given for 1–6.
1. 28; $4 \times 2 = 8$, $4 \times 5 = 20$, and $8 + 20 = 28$
2. 27; $3 \times 4 = 12$, $3 \times 5 = 15$, and $12 + 15 = 27$
3. 31; $2 \times 5 = 10$, $3 \times 7 = 21$, and $10 + 21 = 31$
4. 32; $4 \times 4 = 16$, $2 \times 8 = 16$, and $16 + 16 = 32$
5. Check drawings.
6. 75

Page 99

1. $P = 8 + 3 + 8 + 3 = 22$ units; $A = 8 \times 3 = 24$ square units
2. $P = 6 + 4 + 6 + 4 = 20$ units; $A = 6 \times 4 = 24$ square units
3. Check drawings. Possible answer: rectangles that are 4 by 4 and 7 by 1
4. perimeter: 22 units; area: 28 square units; circle 28
5. area of the triangle

Page 100

Check coloring for 1–4.
Rows should show 9, 10, 8, 5.
5. 18 jars
6. 4 more jars
7. Week 4
8. Week 2

Page 101

1. 20; Count each star as 4 students.
2. 2 students
3. 32 students
4. 10 more students
5. 50 students
6. 4 stars and half of a star
7. Possible answer: There would be another row below 85. It would have half a star next to 80.

Page 102

1. Wednesday
2. Friday
3. 60 shirts
4. 40 more boxes
5. $50
6. 35 boxes of buttons
7. 75 boxes of buttons

Page 103

1. Ben, Anil
2. Crissy
3. 85 votes
4. 135 votes
5. 8 symbols
6. 2 and a half symbols
7. 18 books

Page 104

1. broad jump
2. 6 more students
3. $3
4. 20 inches
5. 24 yards
6. 45 minutes
7. Pool B; 4 m farther

Page 105

1. 3 students
2. 29 students
3. 14 students
4. 6 fewer students
5. 3 more students
6. halfway between 8 and 10

Page 106

1. horizontal
2. the number of students
3. 10 students
4. printmaking
5. clay modeling
6. 165 students
7. $6 \times 8 = 48$; $48 \div 6 = 8$; $48 \div 8 = 6$
8. $56 \div 8 = 7$; $8 \times 7 = 56$; $7 \times 8 = 56$
9. $7 \times 6 = 42$; $42 \div 6 = 7$; $42 \div 7 = 6$

Page 107

1. counting the number sold by 20s
2. January
3. 70 televisions
4. April
5. 70 more televisions
6. 100 televisions
7. Answers will vary. Check graphs.

Page 108

1. 9
2. 21
3. 6
4. 3
5. 10

6. greater than; $16 > 10$
7. bike; Then 8 students would bike. $8 > 7$

Page 109

1. Check graph.
2. Taylor
3. 31 lawns
4. Bar graph and explanation will vary.

Page 110

1. Check graph.
2. $26
3. 5 weeks
4. Bar graph and explanation will vary.

Page 111

Check line plot drawing.
1. 4 shirts
2. $13
3. 17 shirts
4. 12 shirts
5. more than $13; $6 > 5$
6. Yes; no shirts were sold for $15.

Page 112

1. $1\frac{1}{2}$
2. 3
3. $4\frac{1}{2}$
4. $1\frac{1}{4}$
5. $2\frac{3}{4}$
6. $\frac{3}{4}$
7. 2
8. Check drawings and line plot.
9. 5 and 6 inches

Page 113

1. more than 1 liter
2. less than 1 liter
3. about 1 liter
4. less than 1 liter
5. more than 1 liter
6. less than 1 liter
7. Glass D
8. Glass A

Answer Key
Core Skills Math, Grade 3

Page 114

1. 1; more than 1 kilogram; less than 1 kilogram
2. 5; more than 5 kilograms; less than 5 kilograms
3. 2 kilograms
4. 1 kilogram
5. 300 kilograms
6. 2 kilograms

Page 115

1. gram
2. gram
3. kilogram
4. kilograms
5. grams
6. Vic
7. Diego and Mac
8. Cory: 25 kg; Jake: 26 kg
9. a square
10. a circle
11. a triangle
12. triangles

Page 116

1. gram
2. kilogram
3. kilogram
4. kilogram
5. gram
6. gram
7. is more than
8. is the same as
9. more than
10. kilograms

Page 117

1. $145 + 217 = 362$; 362 grams
2. $20 \div 5 = 4$; 4 gas tanks
3. $4 + 2 = 6$; 6 liters
4. $5 \times 40 = 200$; 200 grams
5. $16 \div 4 = 4$; 4 kilograms
6. $12 - 3 = 9$; 9 liters
7. 9 times
8. 23 kilograms

Page 118

1. $\frac{1}{3}, \frac{1}{2}, \frac{1}{3}$
2. $\frac{1}{2}, \frac{1}{3}, \frac{1}{3}$
3. Color $\frac{1}{3}$ of middle and last shapes.
4. Color $\frac{1}{3}$ of last shape.
5. $\frac{1}{2}$

Page 119

1. bottom circle
2. top circle
3. middle circle
Check drawings for 4–5.
6. $\frac{2}{3}$

Page 120

1. $\frac{4}{5}$; four fifths
2. $\frac{2}{4}$; two fourths
3. $\frac{1}{3}$; one third
4. $\frac{3}{4}$; three fourths
5. $\frac{5}{8}$; five eighths
6. $\frac{2}{6}$
7. $\frac{4}{5}$
8. $\frac{4}{4}$
9. $\frac{1}{3}$
10. $\frac{2}{5}$
11. $\frac{4}{6}$
Shade one fourth for 12–14.

Page 121

1. part of a whole
2. part of a group
3. part of a whole
4. Circle second and fourth images.
5. one half
6. one eighth
7. three fourths
8. 4 boxes
9. $\frac{1}{4}$
10. 4 times

Page 122

1. $\frac{2}{5}$
2. $\frac{3}{4}$
3. $\frac{1}{2}$
4. $\frac{5}{8}$
5. $\frac{4}{5}$
6. $\frac{2}{6}$

7. 6
8. $\frac{5}{8}$
9. 32 pieces

Page 123

1. 1 green leaf, 2 yellow leaves
2. 2 orange leaves, 1 red leaf
3. 2 blue leaves, 3 orange leaves
4. 4 purple leaves, 1 yellow leaf
5. 3 green leaves, 1 purple leaf
6. 2 yellow leaves, 2 red leaves
7. 4 red leaves, 2 blue leaves
8. 3 green leaves, 3 purple leaves
9. 3 trees
10. $\frac{3}{4}$

Page 124

1. $\frac{2}{6}$
2. $\frac{2}{5}$
3. $\frac{2}{3}$
4. $\frac{2}{2}$
5. $\frac{0}{5}$
6. $\frac{9}{9}$
7. $\frac{3}{4}$
8. 64 more apples
9. 10 dimes
10. $\frac{1}{10}$

Page 125

Check drawings for 1–2.
1. $\frac{1}{3}, \frac{2}{3}$; draw point at $\frac{1}{3}$
2. $4, \frac{1}{4}, \frac{2}{4}, \frac{3}{4}$; draw point at $\frac{3}{4}$
3. $\frac{2}{8}$
4. $\frac{5}{8}$
5. $\frac{7}{8}$
6. 5 times
7. $\frac{4}{6}$

Page 126

Check drawings for 1–2.
1. 4
2. 2

3. 2
4. 6
5. Yes; possible answer $\frac{4}{4}$
6. Yes; possible answer $\frac{2}{4}$

Page 127

1. true
2. false
3. true
4. false
5. true
6. false
7. 4
8. 1
9. 4
10. 2
11. 1
12. 3
13. 15
14. 40
15. 49
16. 36
17. 54
18. 0
19. 8
20. 9
21. 7
22. 6
23. 6

Page 128

1. $\frac{1}{4}, \frac{2}{8}$
2. $\frac{2}{3}, \frac{4}{6}$
3. $\frac{1}{2}, \frac{2}{4}$
4. $\frac{1}{5}, \frac{2}{10}$
5. $\frac{8}{8}, \frac{4}{4}$
Check drawings for 6–7.
8. You make equivalent fractions.

Page 129

1. 9
2. 3
3. $\frac{2}{6}, \frac{3}{9}$
4. $\frac{2}{8}, \frac{3}{12}$
5. $\frac{4}{8}, \frac{2}{4}$
6. 5 more red balls
7. $\frac{1}{2}$
8. Possible answers: $\frac{1}{2}, \frac{2}{4}$
9. Answers will vary.

Answer Key
Core Skills Math, Grade 3

Page 130

1. 1
2. 1
3. 4
4. $\frac{5}{6}$
5. $\frac{2}{3}$
6. $\frac{1}{3}$
7. $\frac{1}{7}$
8. $\frac{1}{6}$
9. $\frac{1}{2}$
10. $\frac{1}{3}$
11. 8:15 A.M.
12. 5:30 P.M.

Page 131

1. not equal
2. equal
3. not equal
4. $\frac{4}{2}$
5. $\frac{12}{3}$
6. $\frac{12}{4}$
7. $\frac{8}{8}$
8. $\frac{8}{4}$, or 2 miles
9. $\frac{24}{8}$, or 3 miles

Page 132

1. <
2. >
3. >
4. <
5. =
6. >
7. =
8. >
9. <
10. Greta
11. more milk
12. The one cut into 6 pieces has fewer parts, so the pieces are larger.

Page 133

1. >
2. >
3. =
4. <
5. >
6. <
7. >
8. =
9. >

10. <
11. >
12. =
13. <
14. >
15. <
16. John
17. blueberries

Page 134

1. <
2. <
3. >
4. <
5. <
6. >
7. >
8. =
9. <
10. the fruit plate tray
11. yellow

Page 135

1. $\frac{4}{4}, \frac{3}{4}, \frac{1}{4}$
2. $\frac{5}{8}, \frac{2}{8}, \frac{1}{8}$
3. $\frac{1}{2}, \frac{1}{3}, \frac{1}{6}$
4. $\frac{2}{3}, \frac{2}{6}, \frac{2}{8}$
5. $\frac{2}{4}, \frac{3}{4}, \frac{4}{4}$
6. $\frac{2}{6}, \frac{4}{6}, \frac{5}{6}$
7. $\frac{0}{8}, \frac{3}{8}, \frac{7}{8}$
8. $\frac{3}{8}, \frac{3}{6}, \frac{3}{4}$
9. Wednesday
10. green

Page 136

1. 40
2. 80
3. 90
4. 60
5. 30¢
6. 50¢
7. 60¢
8. 90¢
9. 50
10. 60¢
11. 20
12. 50¢
13. 83, 78, 75
14. 71¢, 65¢, 67¢, 69¢
15. 5, 6, 7, 8, 9, 11, 12, 13, 14
16. 45, 54

17. 21–24 pounds
18. Circle the balloons, teddy bear, and boat.

Page 137

1. 800
2. 700
3. 700
4. 800
5. 600
6. 300
7. 800
8. 900
9. 300
10. 500
11. 200
12. 500
13. 350
14. 850
15. 650
16. 11 people
17. about 400 people
18. to the nearest ten; Since ten has a lesser value, the estimation is usually closer.

Page 138

Check point 739 on number line.

1. 700, 800
2. 700, 800
3. 700
4. 360, 400
5. 830, 800
6. 570, 600
7. 210, 200
8. 660, 700
9. 950, 900
10. 760, 800
11. 400, 400
12. 400, 400
13. 400 pounds
14. 220 cups

Page 139

1. 4 oranges
2. 12 ears of corn
3. 8 grapes
4. fewer than 8

Page 140

1. $4 \times 2 = 8$; $8
2. $21 - 16 = 5$; 5
3. $8 + 9 + 7 = 24$; 24
4. $5 \times 4 = 20$; 20
5. Stories will vary. Possible number sentence: $5 \times 3 = 15$

Page 141

1. 8 pencils
2. 6 tables
3. 7 video games
4. 5 gifts
5. 9 movies
6. 6 inches

Page 142

1. Earl: 17; Denise: 25
2. 58 and 65
3. Planet A: 16; Planet B: 18
4. five 3-point, eleven 2-point
5. 5 minutes
6. 130 dB

Page 143

1. addition; 563 miles
2. division; 9 members
3. subtraction; 1,578 more strikeouts
4. multiplication; 40 days
5. addition; the year 2062
6. division; about 7 pints

Answer Key
Core Skills Math, Grade 3